FROM

_____

DATE

_____

100
VERSES
& PRAYERS
❧ FOR ❧
SUCCESSFUL
LEADERS

The quoted ideas expressed in this book (but not Scripture verses) are not, in all cases, exact quotations, as some have been edited for clarity and brevity. In all cases, the author has attempted to maintain the speaker's original intent. In some cases, quoted material for this book was obtained from secondary sources, primarily print media. While every effort was made to ensure the accuracy of these sources, the accuracy cannot be guaranteed. For additions, deletions, corrections, or clarifications in future editions of this text, please write Freeman-Smith.

Scripture quotations are taken from:

The Holy Bible, King James Version

The Holy Bible, New International Version (NIV) Copyright © 1973, 1978, 1984, by International Bible Society. Used by permission of Zondervan Publishing House. All rights reserved.

The Holy Bible, New King James Version (NKJV) Copyright © 1982 by Thomas Nelson, Inc. Used by permission.

The New American Standard Bible®, (NASB) Copyright © 1960, 1962, 1963, 1968, 1971, 1972, 1973, 1975, 1977, 1995 by The Lockman Foundation. Used by permission.

Holy Bible, New Living Translation, (NLT) Copyright © 1996. Used by permission of Tyndale House Publishers, Inc., Wheaton, Illinois 60189. All rights reserved.

The Message (MSG)- This edition issued by contractual arrangement with NavPress, a division of The Navigators, U.S.A. Originally published by NavPress in English as THE MESSAGE: The Bible in Contemporary Language copyright 2002-2003 by Eugene Peterson. All rights reserved.

New Century Version®. (NCV) Copyright © 1987, 1988, 1991 by Word Publishing, a division of Thomas Nelson, Inc. All rights reserved. Used by permission.

The Holman Christian Standard Bible™ (HCSB) Copyright © 1999, 2000, 2001 by Holman Bible Publishers. Used by permission.

Cover Design by Scott Williams/ Richmond & Williams
Page Layout by Bart Dawson

ISBN 978-1-60587-458-6

Printed in the United States of America

15 16 17 18 19—VPI—13 12 11 10 9

100 VERSES & PRAYERS FOR SUCCESSFUL LEADERS

 # INTRODUCTION

There are some Bible verses that are so important, so crucial to the faith, that every Christian leader should know them by heart. This text examines 100 such verses. These Bible promises, which you've probably heard many times before, are short enough, and memorable enough, for you to place safely in your long-term mental database. So, whether you manage a small office or a Fortune 500 corporation, do yourself and your coworkers a favor: study each verse and do your best to place it permanently in your mind and in your heart. When you do, you'll discover that having God's Word in your heart is even better than having a Bible—or 100 management textbooks—on your bookshelf.

I am come that they might have life, and that they might have it more abundantly.

John 10:10 KJV

GREAT LEADERS EXPECT GOD'S ABUNDANCE

The 10th chapter of John tells us that Christ came to earth so that our lives might be filled with abundance. But what, exactly, did Jesus mean when He promised "life . . . more abundantly"? Was He referring to material possessions or financial wealth? Hardly. Jesus offers a different kind of abundance: a spiritual richness that extends beyond the temporal boundaries of this world.

Is material abundance part of God's plan for our lives? Perhaps. But in every circumstance of life, during times of wealth or times of want, God will provide us what we need if we trust Him (Matthew 6). May we, as believers, claim the riches of Christ Jesus every day that we live, and may we share His blessings with all who cross our path.

— A LEADERSHIP TIP —

God wants to shower you and your associates with abundance—your job is to let Him.

God loves you and wants you to experience peace and life—abundant and eternal.

Billy Graham

The only way you can experience abundant life is to surrender your plans to Him.

Charles Stanley

People, places, and things were never meant to give us life. God alone is the author of a fulfilling life.

Gary Smalley & John Trent

Jesus wants Life for us, Life with a capital L.

John Eldredge

— A Leader's Prayer —

Heavenly Father, thank You for the abundant life that is mine through Christ Jesus. Guide me according to Your will, and help me to be a worthy servant in all that I say and do. Give me courage, Lord, to claim the rewards You have promised, and when I do, let the glory be Yours. Amen

Should we accept only good from God and not adversity?

Job 2:10 HCSB

WISE LEADERS LEARN TO ACCEPT THE THINGS THEY CANNOT CHANGE

If you're like most people, you like being in control. Period. You want things to happen according to your wishes and according to your timetable. But sometimes, God has other plans . . . and He always has the final word. Job understood the importance of accepting God's sovereignty in good times and bad . . . and so should you.

The American theologian Reinhold Niebuhr composed a profoundly simple verse that came to be known as the Serenity Prayer: "God, grant me the serenity to accept the things I cannot change, the courage to change the things I can, and the wisdom to know the difference." Niebuhr's words are far easier to recite than they are to live by.

Are you embittered by a personal tragedy that you did not deserve and cannot understand? If so, it's time to make peace with life. It's time to forgive others, and, if necessary, to forgive yourself. It's time to accept the unchangeable past, to embrace the priceless present, and to have faith in the promise of tomorrow. It's time to trust God completely. And it's time to reclaim the peace—His peace—that can and should be yours.

So if you've encountered unfortunate circumstances that are beyond your power to control, accept those circumstances . . . and trust God. When you do, you can be comforted in the knowledge that your Creator is both loving and wise, and that He understands His plans perfectly, even when you don't.

— A Leadership Tip —

When you encounter situations that you cannot change, you must learn the wisdom of acceptance . . . and you must learn to trust God.

Tomorrow's job is fathered by today's acceptance. Acceptance of what, at least for the moment, you cannot alter.

Max Lucado

— A Leader's Prayer —

Lord, when I am discouraged, give me hope. When I am impatient, give me peace. When I face circumstances that I cannot change, give me a spirit of acceptance. In all things great and small, let me trust in You, Dear Lord, knowing that You are the Giver of life and the Giver of all things good, today and forever. Amen

But be doers of the word, and not hearers only, deceiving yourselves.

James 1:22 NKJV

SAVVY LEADERS KNOW THAT ACTIONS SPEAK LOUDER THAN WORDS

The old saying is both familiar and true: actions speak louder than words. And as believers, we must beware: our actions should always give credence to the changes that Christ can make in the lives of those who walk with Him.

God calls upon each of us to act in accordance with His will and with respect for His commandments. If we are to be responsible believers, we must realize that it is never enough simply to hear the instructions of God; we must also live by them. And it is never enough to wait idly by while others do God's work here on earth; we, too, must act. Doing God's work is a responsibility that each of us must bear, and when we do, our loving Heavenly Father rewards our efforts with a bountiful harvest.

Do you seek God's peace and His blessings? Then obey Him. When you're faced with a difficult choice or a powerful temptation, seek God's counsel and trust the counsel He gives. Invite God into your heart and act in accordance with His commandments. When you do, you will be blessed today, and tomorrow, and forever.

— A LEADERSHIP TIP —

Because actions always speak louder than words, it's always a good time to let your actions speak for themselves.

Do noble things, do not dream them all day long.

Charles Kingsley

Logic will not change an emotion, but action will.

Zig Ziglar

We spend our lives dreaming of the future, not realizing that a little of it slips away every day.

Barbara Johnson

We set the sail; God makes the wind.

Anonymous

— A LEADER'S PRAYER —

Dear Lord, I have heard Your Word, and I have felt Your presence in my heart; let me act accordingly. Let my words and deeds serve as a testimony to the changes You have made in my life. Let me praise You, Father, by following in the footsteps of Your Son, and let others see Him through me. Amen

God is our refuge and strength, a very present help in trouble.

Psalm 46:1 NKJV

DURING TOUGH TIMES, WISE LEADERS TRUST GOD AND GET BUSY

The words of Psalm 46:1 promise that God is our refuge, a refuge that we all need. From time to time, all of us face adversity, discouragement, or disappointment. And throughout life, we all must endure life-changing personal losses that leave us breathless. When we do, God stands ready to protect us. Psalm 147 assures us that, "He heals the brokenhearted, and binds their wounds" (v. 3, NIV).

Are you anxious? Take those anxieties to God. Are you troubled? Take your troubles to Him. Does the world seem to be trembling beneath your feet? Seek protection from the One who cannot be moved.

The same God who created the universe stands ready and willing to comfort you and to restore your strength. During life's most difficult days, your Heavenly Father remains steadfast. And, in His own time and according to His master plan, He will heal you if you invite Him into your heart.

— A LEADERSHIP TIP —

When you experience tough times (and you will), a positive attitude makes a big difference in the way you lead your team and tackle your problems.

The sermon of your life in tough times ministers to people more powerfully than the most eloquent speaker.

Bill Bright

Faith is a strong power, mastering any difficulty in the strength of the Lord who made heaven and earth.

Corrie ten Boom

God allows us to experience the low points of life in order to teach us lessons that we could learn in no other way.

C. S. Lewis

— A LEADER'S PRAYER —

Dear Lord, when I face the inevitable challenges of leadership, give me perspective and faith. When I am discouraged, give me the strength to trust Your promises and follow Your will. Then, when I have done my best, Father, let me live with the assurance that You are firmly in control, and that Your love endures forever. Amen

Everyone must be quick to hear, slow to speak, and slow to anger, for man's anger does not accomplish God's righteousness.

James 1:19-20 HCSB

WISE LEADERS UNDERSTAND THE FUTILITY OF ANGER

If you're like most leaders, you know a thing or two (or three) about anger. After all, everybody gets mad occasionally, and you're probably no exception.

Anger is a natural human emotion that is sometimes necessary and appropriate. Even Jesus became angry when confronted with the moneychangers in the temple (Matthew 21). Righteous indignation is an appropriate response to evil, but God does not intend that anger should rule our lives. Far from it.

Temper tantrums are usually unproductive, unattractive, unforgettable, and unnecessary. Perhaps that's why Proverbs 16:32 states that, "Controlling your temper is better than capturing a city" (NCV).

If you've allowed anger to become a regular visitor at your house, you should pray for wisdom, for patience, and for a heart that is so filled with forgiveness that it contains no room for bitterness. God will help you terminate your tantrums if you ask Him—and that's a good thing because anger and peace cannot coexist in the same mind.

If you permit yourself to throw too many tantrums, you will forfeit—at least for now—the peace that might otherwise be yours through Christ. So obey God's Word by turning away from anger today and every day. You'll be glad you did, and so will your family and friends.

— A LEADERSHIP TIP —

Angry words are dangerous to your emotional and spiritual health, not to mention your relationships. So treat anger as an uninvited guest, and usher it away as quickly—and as quietly—as possible.

Anger is the noise of the soul; the unseen irritant of the heart; the relentless invader of silence.

Max Lucado

Life is too short to spend it being angry, bored, or dull.

Barbara Johnson

— A LEADER'S PRAYER —

Lord, sometimes, I am quick to anger and slow to forgive. But I know, Lord, that You seek abundance and peace for my life. Forgiveness is Your commandment; empower me to follow the example of Your Son Jesus who forgave His persecutors. As I turn away from anger, I claim the peace that You intend for my life. Amen

Ask, and it will be given to you; seek, and you will find; knock, and it will be opened to you. For everyone who asks receives, and he who seeks finds, and to him who knocks it will be opened.

Matthew 7:7-8 NKJV

GREAT LEADERS ASK GOD FOR THE THINGS THEY NEED

How often do you ask God for His help and His wisdom? Occasionally? Intermittently? Whenever you experience a crisis? Hopefully not. Hopefully, you've acquired the habit of asking for God's assistance early and often. And hopefully, you have learned to seek His guidance in every aspect of your life.

In Matthew 7, God promises that He will guide you if you let Him. Your job is to let Him. But sometimes, you will be tempted to do otherwise. Sometimes, you'll be tempted to go along with the crowd; other times, you'll be tempted to do things your way, not God's way. When you feel those temptations, resist them.

God has promised that when you ask for His help, He will not withhold it. So ask. Ask Him to meet the needs of your day. Ask Him to lead you, to protect you, and to correct you. And trust the answers He gives.

God stands at the door and waits. When you knock, He opens. When you ask, He answers. Your task, of course, is to seek His guidance prayerfully, confidently, and often.

— A LEADERSHIP TIP —

If you sincerely want to guard your steps, ask for God's help.

By asking in Jesus' name, we're making a request not only in His authority, but also for His interests and His benefit.

Shirley Dobson

Don't be afraid to ask your heavenly Father for anything you need. Indeed, nothing is too small for God's attention or too great for his power.

Dennis Swanberg

— A LEADER'S PRAYER —

Dear Lord, as I lead others, I will ask You for the things I need. In every circumstance, in every season of life, I will come to You in prayer. You know the desires of my heart, Lord; grant them, I ask. Yet not my will, Father, but Your will be done. Amen

Don't be deceived: God is not mocked. For whatever a man sows he will also reap, because the one who sows to his flesh will reap corruption from the flesh, but the one who sows to the Spirit will reap eternal life from the Spirit.

Galatians 6:7-8 HCSB

WISE LEADERS KNOW THAT THEY WILL REAP WHAT THEY SOW

Life is a series of choices. Each day, we make countless decisions that can bring us closer to God. When we live according to God's commandments, we earn for ourselves the abundance and peace that He intends for our lives. But, when we turn our backs upon God by disobeying Him, we bring needless suffering upon ourselves and our families.

Are you the kind of leader who seeks God's peace and His blessings? Then obey Him. When you're faced with a difficult choice or a powerful temptation, seek God's counsel and trust the counsel He gives. Invite God into your heart and live according to His commandments. When you do, you will be blessed today, and tomorrow, and forever.

— A LEADERSHIP TIP —

Nature gives man corn, but he must grind it; God gives man a will, but he must make the right choices.

Fulton J. Sheen

Don't worry about what you do not understand. Worry about what you do understand in the Bible but do not live by.

Corrie ten Boom

More depends on my walk than my talk.

D. L. Moody

Our response to God determines His response to us.

Henry Blackaby

When you discover the Christian way, you discover your own way as a person.

E. Stanley Jones

Christianity says we were created by a righteous God to flourish and be exhilarated in a righteous environment. God has "wired" us in such a way that the more righteous we are, the more we'll actually enjoy life.

Bill Hybels

— A LEADER'S PRAYER —

Lord, because I am a leader, I am a role model. I pray that my actions will always be consistent with my beliefs. I know that my deeds speak more loudly than my words. May every step that I take reflect Your truth and love, and may others be drawn to You because of my words and my deeds. Amen

All bitterness, anger and wrath, insult and slander must be removed from you, along with all wickedness. And be kind and compassionate to one another, forgiving one another, just as God also forgave you in Christ.

Ephesians 4:31-32 HCSB

WISE LEADERS UNDERSTAND THE FUTILITY OF BITTERNESS

In the fourth chapter of Ephesians, we are warned about the dangers of bitterness, and with good reason. Bitterness is a spiritual sickness. It will consume your soul; it is dangerous to your emotional health. It can destroy you if you let it . . . so don't let it!

If you are caught up in intense feelings of anger or resentment, you know all too well the destructive power of these emotions. How can you rid yourself of these feelings? First, you must prayerfully ask God to cleanse your heart. Then, you must learn to catch yourself whenever thoughts of bitterness or hatred begin to attack you. Your challenge is this: You must learn to resist negative thoughts before they hijack your emotions.

When you learn to direct your thoughts toward more positive (and rational) topics, you'll be protected from the spiritual and emotional consequences of bitterness . . . and you'll be wiser, healthier, and happier, too.

— A Leadership Tip —

You can never fully enjoy the present if you're bitter about the past. Instead of living in the past, make peace with it . . . and move on.

Bitterness is the greatest barrier to friendship with God.

Rick Warren

Be patient and understanding. Life is too short to be vengeful or malicious.

Phillips Brooks

Bitterness only makes suffering worse and closes the spiritual channels through which God can pour His grace.

Warren Wiersbe

— A Leader's Prayer —

Heavenly Father, free me from anger and bitterness. When I am angry, I cannot feel the peace that You intend for my life. When I am bitter, I cannot sense Your presence. Keep me mindful that forgiveness is Your commandment. Let me turn away from bitterness and instead claim the spiritual abundance that You offer through the gift of Your Son. Amen

Rejoice in the Lord always. Again I will say, rejoice!

Philippians 4:4 NKJV

GREAT LEADERS CELEBRATE LIFE

Are you living a life of agitation, consternation, or celebration? If you're a believer, it should most certainly be the latter. With Christ as your Savior, every day should be a time of celebration.

Oswald Chambers correctly observed, "Joy is the great note all throughout the Bible." C. S. Lewis echoed that thought when he wrote, "Joy is the serious business of heaven." But, even the most dedicated Christians can, on occasion, forget to celebrate each day for what it is: a priceless gift from God.

Today, celebrate the life that God has given you. Today, put a smile on your face, kind words on your lips, and a song in your heart. Be generous with your praise and free with your encouragement. And then, when you have celebrated life to the fullest, invite your friends to do likewise. After all, this is God's day, and He has given us clear instructions for its use. We are commanded to rejoice and be glad. So, with no further ado, let the celebration begin.

— A Leadership Tip —

Every day should be a cause for celebration. By celebrating the gift of life, you protect your heart from the dangers of pessimism, regret, and bitterness.

Joy is the direct result of having God's perspective on our daily lives and the effect of loving our Lord enough to obey His commands and trust His promises.

Bill Bright

A life of intimacy with God is characterized by joy.

Oswald Chambers

If you can forgive the person you were, accept the person you are, and believe in the person you will become, you are headed for joy. So celebrate your life.

Barbara Johnson

— A Leader's Prayer —

Dear Lord, You have given me so many reasons to celebrate. Today, let me choose an attitude of cheerfulness. Let me be a joyful Christian leader, Lord, quick to laugh and slow to anger. Let me praise You, Lord, and give thanks for Your blessings. Today is Your creation; let me celebrate it . . . and You. Amen

VERSE 10

I the Lord do not change.

Malachi 3:6 HCSB

WISE LEADERS UNDERSTAND THAT THE WORLD CHANGES BUT GOD DOES NOT

We live in a world that is always changing, but we worship a God who never changes—thank goodness! That means that we can be comforted in the knowledge that our Heavenly Father is the rock that simply cannot be moved.

The next time you face difficult circumstances, tough times, unfair treatment, or unwelcome changes, remember that some things never change—things like the love that you feel in your heart for your family and friends . . . and the love that God feels for you. So, instead of worrying too much about life's inevitable challenges, focus your energies on finding solutions. Have faith in your own abilities, do your best to solve your problems, and leave the rest up to God.

— A LEADERSHIP TIP —
Failure is not fatal, but failure to change might be.

John Wooden

More often than not, when something looks like it's the absolute end, it is really the beginning.

Charles Swindoll

In a world kept chaotic by change, you will eventually discover, as I have, that this is one of the most precious qualities of the God we are looking for: He doesn't change.

Bill Hybels

Mere change is not growth. Growth is the synthesis of change and continuity, and where there is no continuity there is no growth.

C. S. Lewis

The secret of contentment in the midst of change is found in having roots in the changeless Christ—the same yesterday, today and forever.

Ed Young

With God, it isn't who you were that matters; it's who you are becoming.

Liz Curtis Higgs

— A Leader's Prayer —

Dear Lord, our world is constantly changing. When I face the inevitable transitions of life, I will turn to You for strength and assurance. Thank You, Father, for love that is unchanging and everlasting. Amen

VERSE 11

A merry heart does good, like medicine.

Proverbs 17:22 NKJV

WISE LEADERS UNDERSTAND THAT IT'S IMPORTANT TO BE CHEERFUL

Cheerfulness is a gift that we give to others and to ourselves. And, as believers who have been saved by a risen Christ, why shouldn't we be cheerful? The answer, of course, is that we have every reason to honor our Savior with joy in our hearts, smiles on our faces, and words of celebration on our lips.

Few things in life are more sad, or, for that matter, more absurd, than grumpy Christians. Christ promises us lives of abundance and joy if we accept His love and His grace. Yet sometimes, even the most righteous among us are beset by fits of ill temper and frustration. During these moments, we may not feel like turning our thoughts and prayers to Christ, but if we seek to gain perspective and peace, that's precisely what we must do.

Are you a cheerful Christian? You should be! And what is the best way to attain the joy that is rightfully yours? By giving Christ what is rightfully His: your heart, your soul, and your life.

— A Leadership Tip —

Cheerfulness is an attitude that is highly contagious. Remember that cheerfulness starts at the top—a cheerful organization usually begins with a cheerful leader.

Be assured, my dear friend, that it is no joy to God in seeing you with a dreary countenance.

C. H. Spurgeon

Christ can put a spring in your step and a thrill in your heart. Optimism and cheerfulness are products of knowing Christ.

Billy Graham

God is good, and heaven is forever. And if those two facts don't cheer you up, nothing will.

Marie T. Freeman

— A Leader's Prayer —

Make me a cheerful leader, Lord. Let me celebrate the day that You have given me, and let me celebrate Your Son. Let me speak words of encouragement and hope to all who cross my path, and let others see the joy and thanksgiving that I feel in my heart for Your priceless gift to the world: Christ Jesus. Amen

*I have set before you life and death, blessing and curse.
Choose life so that you and your descendants may live,
love the Lord your God, obey Him, and remain faithful
to Him. For He is your life, and He will prolong your
life in the land the Lord swore to give to your fathers
Abraham, Isaac, and Jacob.*

Deuteronomy 30:19-20 HCSB

WISE LEADERS UNDERSTAND
THE IMPORTANCE OF MAKING
GOOD CHOICES

From the instant we wake in the morning until
the moment we nod off to sleep at night, we make
countless decisions: decisions about the things we
do, decisions about the words we speak, and decisions about the thoughts we choose to think. Simply put, the quality of those decisions determines
the quality of our lives.

As believers who have been saved by a loving
and merciful God, we have every reason to make
wise choices. Yet sometimes, amid the inevitable
hustle and bustle of life here on earth, we allow
ourselves to behave in ways that we know are displeasing to God. When we do, we forfeit—albeit
temporarily—the joy and the peace that we might
otherwise experience through Him.

As you examine your own leadership style,
consider how many things in this life you can

control: your thoughts, your words, your priorities, and your actions, for starters. And then, if you sincerely want to discover God's purpose for your life, make choices that are pleasing to Him. He deserves no less . . . and neither do you.

— A LEADERSHIP TIP —

Every day you make hundreds of choices . . . and the quality of those choices determines the quality of your day, your career, and your life.

Every time you make a choice, you are turning the central part of you, the part that chooses, into something a little different from what it was before.

C. S. Lewis

Life is pretty much like a cafeteria line—it offers us many choices, both good and bad. The Christian must have a spiritual radar that detects the difference not only between bad and good but also among good, better, and best.

Dennis Swanberg

— A LEADER'S PRAYER —

Heavenly Father, I have many choices to make. Help me choose wisely as I follow in the footsteps of Your only begotten Son. Amen

I have learned to be content in whatever circumstances I am.

Philippians 4:11 HCSB

FINDING CONTENTMENT

The preoccupation with happiness and contentment is an ever-present theme in the modern world. We are bombarded with messages that tell us where to find peace and pleasure in a world that worships materialism and wealth. But, lasting contentment is not found in material possessions; genuine contentment is a spiritual gift from God to those who trust in Him and follow His commandments.

Where do we find contentment? If we don't find it in God, we will never find it anywhere else. But, if we put our faith and our trust in Him, we will be blessed with an inner peace that is beyond human understanding. When God dwells at the center of our lives, peace and contentment will belong to us just as surely as we belong to God.

— A LEADERSHIP TIP —

True contentment is a real and active virtue—not only affirmative but creative. It is the power of getting out of any situation all there is in it.

G. K. Chesterton

God would rather have a man on the wrong side of the fence than on the fence. The worst enemies of apostles are not the opposers but the appeasers.

Vance Havner

God is able to do anything He pleases with one ordinary person fully consecrated to Him.

Henry Blackaby and Claude King

We become whatever we are committed to.

Rick Warren

Commitment doesn't come easy, but when you're fighting for something you believe in, the struggle is worth it.

John Maxwell

When we give ourselves wholly to God, He takes from our meager reserves and gives back from infinity. What a marvelous exchange!

Shirley Dobson

— A Leader's Prayer —

Heavenly Father, let me be a leader who strives to do Your will here on earth, and as I do, let me find contentment and balance. Let me live in the light of Your will and Your priorities for my life, and when I have done my best, Lord, give me the wisdom to place my faith and my trust in You. Amen

And if a kingdom be divided against itself, that kingdom cannot stand. And if a house be divided against itself, that house cannot stand.

Mark 3:24-25 KJV

GREAT LEADERS KNOW THAT COOPERATION PAYS

Have you and your associates learned the subtle art of cooperation? If so, you have learned the wisdom of "give and take," not the foolishness of "me first." Cooperation is the art of compromising on many little things while keeping your eye on one big thing: your collective goals.

But here's a word of warning: if you're like most folks in positions of leadership, you're probably a little bit headstrong: you probably want most things done in a fashion resembling the popular song "My Way." But, if you are observant, you will notice that those people who always insist upon "my way or the highway" usually end up with "the highway."

A better strategy for all concerned (including you) is to abandon the search for "my way" and search instead for "our way." The happiest and most productive organizations are those in which everybody learns how to "give and take" . . . with the emphasis on "give."

— A LEADERSHIP TIP —

When you and your associates work as a team, you accomplish more. When you don't work as a team, you accomplish less. So it pays to cooperate.

Cooperation is a two-way street, but for too many couples, it's the road less traveled.

Marie T. Freeman

One person working together doesn't accomplish much. Success is the result of people pulling together to meet common goals.

John Maxwell

Teamwork makes the dream work.

John Maxwell

Coming together is a beginning. Keeping together is progress. Working together is success.

John Maxwell

— A LEADER'S PRAYER —

Dear Lord, help me learn to be kind, courteous, and cooperative with my family, with my associates, with my friends, and with all who cross my path. Amen

Be strong and courageous, and do the work. Don't be afraid or discouraged, for the Lord God, my God, is with you. He won't leave you or forsake you.

1 Chronicles 28:20 HCSB

GREAT LEADERS ARE COURAGEOUS

Christians have every reason to live—and to lead—courageously. After all, the ultimate battle has already been won on the cross at Calvary. But even dedicated Christians may find their courage tested by the inevitable disappointments and fears that visit the lives of believers and non-believers alike.

When you find yourself worried about the challenges of today or the uncertainties of tomorrow, you must ask yourself whether or not you are ready to place your concerns and your life in God's all-powerful, all-knowing, all-loving hands. If the answer to that question is yes—as it should be—then you can draw courage today from the source of strength that never fails: your Heavenly Father.

— A LEADERSHIP TIP —

We are not weak if we make proper use of those means which the God of nature hath placed in our power. The battle, sir, is not to the strong alone; it is to the vigilant, the active, the brave.

Patrick Henry

Courage is not simply one of the virtues, but the form of every virtue at the testing point, which means, at the point of highest reality. A chastity or honesty or mercy which yields to danger will be chaste or honest or merciful only on conditions. Pilate was merciful till it became risky.

C. S. Lewis

If a person fears God, he or she has no reason to fear anything else. On the other hand, if a person does not fear God, then fear becomes a way of life.

Beth Moore

Courage is contagious.

Billy Graham

Daniel looked into the face of God and would not fear the face of a lion.

C. H. Spurgeon

The truth of Christ brings assurance and so removes the former problem of fear and uncertainty.

A. W. Tozer

— A Leader's Prayer —

Dear Lord, when I am fearful or worried, give me courage, perspective, and wisdom. In every circumstance, I will trust You to guide me and protect me, now and forever. Amen

Are there those among you who are truly wise and understanding? Then they should show it by living right and doing good things with a gentleness that comes from wisdom.

James 3:13 NCV

WISE LEADERS KNOW THAT IT PAYS TO BE COURTEOUS

Did Christ instruct us in matters of etiquette and courtesy? Of course He did. Christ's instructions are clear: "In everything, therefore, treat people the same way you want them to treat you, for this is the Law and the Prophets" (Matthew 7:12 NASB). Jesus did not say, "In some things, treat people as you wish to be treated." And, He did not say, "From time to time, treat others with kindness." Christ said that we should treat others as we wish to be treated in every aspect of our daily lives. This, of course, is a tall order indeed, but as Christians, we are commanded to do our best.

Today, be a little kinder than necessary to family members, friends, associates, coworkers, and total strangers. And, as you consider all the things that Christ has done in your life, honor Him with your words and with your deeds. He expects no less, and He deserves no less.

— A Leadership Tip —

If you disagree, do so without being disagreeable; if you're angry, hold your tongue; if you're frustrated or tired, don't argue . . . take a coffee break.

Only the courteous can love, but it is love that makes them courteous.

C. S. Lewis

When you extend hospitality to others, you're not trying to impress people; you're trying to reflect God to them.

Max Lucado

Reach out and care for someone who needs the touch of hospitality. The time you spend caring today will be a love gift that will blossom into the fresh joy of God's Spirit in the future.

Emilie Barnes

— A Leader's Prayer —

Guide me, Lord, to treat all those I meet with courtesy and respect. You have created each person in Your own image; let me honor those who cross my path with the dignity that You have bestowed upon them. We are all Your children, Lord; let me show kindness to all. Amen

VERSE 17

Don't criticize one another, brothers. He who criticizes a brother or judges his brother criticizes the law and judges the law. But if you judge the law, you are not a doer of the law but a judge.

James 4:11 HCSB

WISE LEADERS REFRAIN FROM NEEDLESS CRITICISM

From experience, we know that it is easier to criticize than to correct; we understand that it is easier to find faults than solutions; and we realize that excessive criticism is usually destructive, not productive. Yet the urge to criticize others remains a powerful temptation for most of us.

In verse 11, James issues a clear warning: "Don't criticize one another, brothers." Undoubtedly, James understood the paralyzing power of chronic negativity, and so should we. Our task, as obedient believers, is to break the twin habits of negative thinking and critical speech.

Negativity is highly contagious: we give it to others who, in turn, give it back to us. This cycle can be broken by positive thoughts, heartfelt prayers, and encouraging words. As thoughtful servants of a loving God, we can use the transforming power of Christ's love to break the chains of negativity.

— A Leadership Tip —

If you're too critical of other people—or of yourself—it's time to become more forgiving and less judgmental.

The business of finding fault is very easy, and that of doing better is very difficult.

Francis de Sales

We would all much better mend our ways if we were as ready to pray for one another as we are to offer one another reproach and rebuke.

Thomas More

The scrutiny we give other people should be for ourselves.

Oswald Chambers

Being critical of others, including God, is one way we try to avoid facing and judging our own sins.

Warren Wiersbe

— A Leader's Prayer —

Help me, Lord, rise above the need to criticize others. May my own shortcomings humble me, and may I always be a source of genuine encouragement to my family, to my associates, and to my friends. Amen

We are hard pressed on every side, yet not crushed; we are perplexed, but not in despair.

2 Corinthians 4:8 NKJV

GREAT LEADERS ARE NOT EASILY DISCOURAGED

We Christians have many reasons to celebrate. God is in His heaven; Christ has risen, and we are the sheep of His flock. Yet sometimes, even the most devout believers may become discouraged. After all, we live in a world where expectations can be high and demands can be even higher.

When we fail to meet the expectations of others (or, for that matter, the expectations that we have for ourselves), we may be tempted to abandon hope. But God has other plans. He knows exactly how He intends to use us. Our task is to remain faithful until He does.

If you become discouraged with the direction of your day, your career, or your life, turn your thoughts and prayers to God. He is a God of possibility, not negativity. He will help you count your blessings instead of your hardships. And then, with a renewed spirit of optimism and hope, you can properly thank your Father in heaven for His blessings, for His love, and for His Son.

— A Leadership Tip —

Men's best successes come after their disappointments.

Henry Ward Beecher

The next time you're disappointed, don't panic and don't give up. Just be patient and let God remind you he's still in control.

Max Lucado

If your hopes are being disappointed just now, it means that they are being purified.

Oswald Chambers

Though our pain and our disappointment and the details of our suffering may differ, there is an abundance of God's grace and peace available to each of us.

Charles Swindoll

— A Leader's Prayer —

Dear Lord, when I face the inevitable disappointments of life, remind me that You are in control. You are the Giver of all good things, Father, and You will bless me today, tomorrow, and forever. Amen

Therefore, get your minds ready for action, being self-disciplined, and set your hope completely on the grace to be brought to you at the revelation of Jesus Christ.

1 Peter 1:13 HCSB

GREAT LEADERS HAVE SELF-DISCIPLINE

God's Word reminds us again and again that our Creator expects us to lead disciplined lives. God doesn't reward laziness, misbehavior, or apathy. To the contrary, He expects us to behave with dignity and discipline. But ours is a world in which dignity and discipline are often in short supply.

We live in a world in which leisure is glorified and indifference is often glamorized. But God has other plans. God gives us talents, and He expects us to use them. But it is not always easy to cultivate those talents. Sometimes, we must invest countless hours (or, in some cases, many years) honing our skills. And that's perfectly okay with God, because He understands that self-discipline is a blessing, not a burden.

When we pause to consider how much work needs to be done, we realize that self-discipline is not simply a proven way to get ahead, it's also an integral part of God's plan for our lives. If we genuinely seek to be faithful stewards of our time, our talents, and our resources, we must adopt a disciplined approach to life. Otherwise, our talents are wasted and our resources are squandered.

Life's greatest rewards seldom fall into our laps; to the contrary, our greatest accomplishments usually require work, perseverance, and discipline. May we, as disciplined believers and Christian leaders, be willing to work for the rewards we so earnestly desire.

— A Leadership Tip —
If you're a disciplined leader, you'll earn big rewards. If you're undisciplined, you won't.

Simply stated, self-discipline is obedience to God's Word and willingness to submit everything in life to His will, for His ultimate glory.

John MacArthur

You can't climb the ladder of life with your hands in your pockets.

Barbara Johnson

— A Leader's Prayer —
Dear Lord, I want to be a disciplined leader. Let me use my time wisely, let me obey Your commandments faithfully, and let me worship You joyfully, today and every day. Amen

For this very reason, make every effort to supplement your faith with goodness, goodness with knowledge, knowledge with self-control, self-control with endurance, endurance with godliness.

2 Peter 1:5-6 HCSB

WISE LEADERS RISE ABOVE THEIR NEGATIVE EMOTIONS

Over and over again, the Bible instructs us to live by faith. Yet sometimes, despite our best intentions, negative feelings can rob us of the peace and abundance that would otherwise be ours through Christ. When anger or anxiety separates us from the spiritual blessings that God has in store, we must rethink our priorities. And we must place faith above feelings.

Human emotions are highly variable, decidedly unpredictable, and often unreliable. Our emotions are like the weather, only sometimes far more fickle. So we must learn to live by faith, not by the ups and downs of our own emotional roller coasters.

Who's pulling your emotional strings? Are you allowing highly emotional people or highly-charged situations to dictate your moods and distract your focus? Or are you wiser than that?

Sometime during the coming day, you may encounter a tough situation or a difficult person. And as a result, you may be gripped by a strong negative emotion. Distrust it. Reign it in. Test it. And turn it over to God.

Your emotions will inevitably change; God will not. So trust Him completely. When you do, you'll be surprised at how quickly those negative feelings can evaporate into thin air.

— A Leadership Tip —

Here are the facts: God's love is real; His peace is real; His support is real; and, He wants you to follow in the footsteps of His Son. Don't ever let your emotions obscure these facts.

I may no longer depend on pleasant impulses to bring me before the Lord. I must rather respond to principles I know to be right, whether I feel them to be enjoyable or not.

Jim Elliot

— A Leader's Prayer —

Heavenly Father, You are my strength and my refuge. As I journey through this day, I will encounter events that cause me emotional distress. Lord, when I am troubled, let me turn to You. Keep me steady, Lord, and in those difficult moments, renew a right spirit inside my heart. Amen

But encourage each other daily, while it is still called to-day, so that none of you is hardened by sin's deception.

Hebrews 3:13 HCSB

WISE LEADERS KNOW THE POWER OF ENCOURAGEMENT

Life is a team sport, and all of us need occasional pats on the back from our teammates. As Christians, we are called upon to spread the Good News of Christ, and we are also called to spread a message of encouragement and hope to the world.

Whether you realize it or not, many people whom you lead are in desperate need of a smile or an encouraging word. The world can be a difficult place, and countless friends and family members may be troubled by the challenges of everyday life. Since you don't always know who needs your help, the best strategy is to try to encourage all the people who cross your path. So today, be a world-class source of encouragement to everyone you meet. Never has the need been greater.

— A LEADERSHIP TIP —

Outstanding leaders go out of their way to boost the self-esteem of their personnel. If people believe in themselves, it's amazing what they can accomplish.

Sam Walton

Make it a rule, and pray to God to help you to keep it, never to lie down at night without being able to say: "I have made at least one human being a little wiser, a little happier, or a little better this day."

Charles Kingsley

I can usually sense that a leading is from the Holy Spirit when it calls me to humble myself, to serve somebody, to encourage somebody, or to give something away. Very rarely will the evil one lead us to do those kind of things.

Bill Hybels

God is still in the process of dispensing gifts, and He uses ordinary individuals like us to develop those gifts in other people.

Howard Hendricks

He climbs highest who helps another up.

Zig Ziglar

— A LEADER'S PRAYER —

Dear Lord, let me celebrate the accomplishments of others. Make me a source of genuine, lasting encouragement to my family and to my associates. And let my words and deeds be worthy of Your Son, the One who gives me strength and salvation, this day and for all eternity. Amen

But those who wait on the LORD shall renew their strength; they shall mount up with wings like eagles, they shall run and not be weary, they shall walk and not faint.

Isaiah 40:31 NKJV

WISE LEADERS DRAW STRENGTH FROM THE LORD

All of us have moments when we feel exhausted. All of us suffer through tough times, difficult days, and perplexing periods of our lives. Thankfully, God promises to give us comfort and strength if we turn to Him.

If you're a person with too many demands and too few hours in which to meet them, it's probably time to examine your priorities while you pare down your daily to-do list. While you're at it, take time to focus upon God and His love for you. Then, ask Him for the wisdom to prioritize your life and the strength to fulfill your responsibilities. God will give you the energy to do the most important things on today's to-do list if you ask Him.

— A LEADERSHIP TIP —

Within us there are wells of thought and dynamos of energy which are not suspected until emergencies arise.

Thomas J. Watson

God is the One who provides our strength, not only to cope with the demands of the day, but also to rise above them. May we look to Him for the strength to soar.

Jim Gallery

God does not dispense strength and encouragement like a druggist fills your prescription. The Lord doesn't promise to give us something to take so we can handle our weary moments. He promises us Himself. That is all. And that is enough.

Charles Swindoll

Worry does not empty tomorrow of its sorrow; it empties today of its strength.

Corrie ten Boom

Sometimes I think spiritual and physical strength is like manna: you get just what you need for the day, no more.

Suzanne Dale Ezell

— A LEADER'S PRAYER —

Lord, let me find my strength in You. When I am weary, give me rest. When I feel overwhelmed, let me look to You for my priorities. Let Your power be my power, Lord, and let Your way be my way, today and forever. Amen

VERSE 23

Whatever you do, do it enthusiastically, as something done for the Lord and not for men.

Colossians 3:23 HCSB

ENTHUSIASM NOW

Do you see each day as a glorious opportunity to serve God and to do His will? Are you enthused about life and your leadership opportunities, or do you struggle through each day giving scarcely a thought to God's blessings? Are you constantly praising God for His gifts, and are you sharing His Good News with the world? And are you excited about the possibilities for service that God has placed before you, whether at home, at work, at church, or at school? You should be.

You are the recipient of Christ's sacrificial love. Accept it enthusiastically and share it fervently. Jesus deserves your enthusiasm; the world deserves it; and you deserve the experience of sharing it.

— A LEADERSHIP TIP —
We act as though comfort and luxury were the chief requirements of life, when all we need to make us really happy is something to be enthusiastic about.

Charles Kingsley

Don't take hold of a thing unless you want that thing to take hold of you.

E. Stanley Jones

Enthusiasm, like the flu, is contagious—we get it from one another.

Barbara Johnson

Wherever you are, be all there. Live to the hilt every situation you believe to be the will of God.

Jim Elliot

One of the great needs in the church today is for every Christian to become enthusiastic about his faith in Jesus Christ.

Billy Graham

When we wholeheartedly commit ourselves to God, there is nothing mediocre or run-of-the-mill about us. To live for Christ is to be passionate about our Lord and about our lives.

Jim Gallery

— A Leader's Prayer —

Dear Lord, I know that others are watching the way that I live my life. Help me to be an enthusiastic Christian leader with a faith that is contagious. Amen.

So rid yourselves of all wickedness, all deceit, hypocrisy, envy, and all slander.

1 Peter 2:1 HCSB

WISE LEADERS UNDERSTAND THAT ENVY IS DANGEROUS

Because we are frail, imperfect human beings, we are sometimes envious of others. But God's Word warns us that envy is sin. Thus, we must guard ourselves against the natural tendency to feel resentment and jealousy when other people experience good fortune.

As believers, we have absolutely no reason to be envious of any people on earth. After all, as Christians we are already recipients of the greatest gift in all creation: God's grace. We have been promised the gift of eternal life through God's only begotten Son, and we must count that gift as our most precious possession.

Rather than succumbing to the sin of envy, we should focus on the marvelous things that God has done for us—starting with Christ's sacrifice. And we must refrain from preoccupying ourselves with the blessings that God has chosen to give others.

So here's a surefire formula for a happier, healthier life: Count your own blessings and let your neighbors count theirs. It's the godly way to live and the best way to lead.

— A LEADERSHIP TIP —

As a moth gnaws a garment, so does envy consume a man.

St. John Chrysostom

What God asks, does, or requires of others is not my business; it is His.

Kay Arthur

When you worry about what you don't have, you won't be able to enjoy what you do have.

Charles Swindoll

How can you possess the miseries of envy when you possess in Christ the best of all portions?

C. H. Spurgeon

Discontent dries up the soul.

Elisabeth Elliot

— A LEADER'S PRAYER —

Dear Lord, today I will be grateful for my blessings, and I won't be envious of the blessings You've given to others. Amen

For God so loved the world, that he gave his only begotten Son, that whosoever believeth in him should not perish, but have everlasting life.

John 3:16 KJV

THE GIFT OF ETERNAL LIFE

John 3:16 is, quite possibly, the most widely recognized sentence in the entire Bible. But even if you memorized this verse many years ago, you still need to make sure it's a verse that you can recite by heart.

John 3:16 makes this promise: If you believe in Jesus, you will live forever with Him in heaven. It's an amazing promise, and it's the cornerstone of the Christian faith.

Eternal life is not an event that begins when you die. Eternal life begins when you invite Jesus into your heart right here on earth. So it's important to remember that God's plans for you are not limited to the ups and downs of everyday life. If you've allowed Jesus to reign over your heart, you've already begun your eternal journey.

As mere mortals, our vision for the future, like our lives here on earth, is limited. God's vision is not burdened by such limitations: His plans extend throughout all eternity.

Let us praise the Creator for His priceless gift, and let us share the Good News with all who cross our paths. We return our Father's love by accepting His grace and by sharing His message and His love. When we do, we are blessed here on earth and throughout all eternity.

— A Leadership Tip —

God offers you life abundant and life eternal. If you have not accepted His gift, the appropriate moment to do so is now.

Teach us to set our hopes on heaven, to hold firmly to the promise of eternal life, so that we can withstand the struggles and storms of this world.

Max Lucado

Your choice to either receive or reject the Lord Jesus Christ will determine where you spend eternity.

Anne Graham Lotz

All that is not eternal is eternally out of date.

C. S. Lewis

— A Leader's Prayer —

Lord, You have given me the priceless gift of eternal life through Your Son Jesus. Keep the hope of heaven fresh in my heart. While I am in this world, help me to pass through it with faith in my heart and praise on my lips for You. Amen

Be an example to the believers in word, in conduct, in love, in spirit, in faith, in purity.

1 Timothy 4:12 NKJV

GREAT LEADERS SET THE RIGHT KIND OF EXAMPLE

Whether we like it or not, all of us are role models. Our friends, families, and coworkers watch our actions and, as followers of Christ, we are obliged to act accordingly.

What kind of example are you? Are you the kind of leader whose life serves as a genuine example of righteousness? Are you a leader whose behavior serves as a positive role model for others? Are you the kind of person whose actions, day in and day out, are based upon kindness, faithfulness, and a love for the Lord? If so, you are not only blessed by God, but you are also a powerful force for good in a world that desperately needs positive influences such as yours.

We live in a dangerous, temptation-filled world. That's why you encounter so many opportunities to stray from God's commandments. Resist those temptations! When you do, you'll earn God's blessings and you'll serve as a positive role model for your family and friends.

Corrie ten Boom advised, "Don't worry about what you do not understand. Worry about what you do understand in the Bible but do not live by." And that's sound advice because our families and friends are watching . . . and so, for that matter, is God.

— A LEADERSHIP TIP —

God wants you to be a positive role model. And that's what you should want, too.

The sermon of your life in tough times ministers to people more powerfully than the most eloquent speaker.

Bill Bright

Your life is destined to be an example. The only question is "what kind?"

Marie T. Freeman

We must mirror God's love in the midst of a world full of hatred. We are the mirrors of God's love, so we may show Jesus by our lives.

Corrie ten Boom

— A LEADER'S PRAYER —

Lord, make me a worthy example to my family, to my friends, and to my coworkers. And, let my words and my deeds serve as a testimony to the changes You have made in my life. Let me praise You, Father, by following in the footsteps of Your Son, and let others see Him through me. Amen

Therefore, get your minds ready for action, being self-disciplined, and set your hope completely on the grace to be brought to you at the revelation of Jesus Christ.

1 Peter 1:13 HCSB

GREAT LEADERS DON'T MAKE EXCUSES

We live in a world where excuses are everywhere. And it's precisely because excuses are so numerous that they are also so ineffective. When we hear the words, "I'm sorry but . . . ," most of us know exactly what is to follow: The Big Excuse. The dog ate the homework. Traffic was terrible. It's the company's fault. The boss is to blame. The equipment is broken. We're out of that. And so forth, and so on.

Because we humans are such creative excuse-makers, all of the really good excuses have already been taken. In fact, the high-quality excuses have been used, reused, overused, and abused. That's why excuses don't work—we've heard them all before.

So, if you're wasting your time trying to portray yourself as a victim (and weakening your character in the process), or if you're trying to concoct a new and improved excuse, don't bother. Excuses don't work, and while you're inventing them, neither do you.

— A Leadership Tip —

A man may make mistakes, but he isn't a failure until he starts blaming someone else.

John Wooden

Replace your excuses with fresh determination.

Charles Swindoll

We need to stop focusing on our lacks and stop giving out excuses and start looking at and listening to Jesus.

Anne Graham Lotz

Rationalization: It's what we do when we substitute false explanations for true reasons, when we cloud our actual motives with a smoke screen of nice-sounding excuses.

Charles Swindoll

An excuse is only the skin of a reason stuffed with a lie.

Vance Havner

— A Leader's Prayer —

Heavenly Father, how easy it is to make excuses. But, I want to be a leader who accomplishes important work for You. Help me, Father, to strive for excellence, not excuses. Amen

Choose for yourselves today the one you will worship . . . . As for me and my family, we will worship the Lord.

Joshua 24:15 HCSB

LEADING YOUR FAMILY BY SERVING GOD

In a world filled with countless obligations and frequent frustrations, we may be tempted to take our families for granted. But God intends otherwise.

Our families are precious gifts from our Father in heaven. If we are to be the righteous men and women who God intends, we must care for our loved ones by making time for them, even when the demands of the day are great.

Undeniably, these are difficult days for Christian households: never have distractions and temptations been greater. But, thankfully, God is bigger than all our challenges.

No family is perfect, and neither is yours. But, despite the inevitable challenges, obligations, and hurt feelings of family life, your clan is God's blessing to you. That little band of men, women, kids, and babies is a priceless treasure on temporary loan from the Father above. Give thanks to the Giver for the gift of family . . . and act accordingly.

— A Leadership Tip —

Your family is a precious gift from above, a gift that should be treasured, nurtured, and loved.

More than any other single factor in a person's formative years, family life forges character.

John Maxwell

A family is a place where principles are hammered and honed on the anvil of everyday living.

Charles Swindoll

Calm and peaceful, the home should be the one place where people are certain they will be welcomed, received, protected, and loved.

Ed Young

Every Christian family ought to be, as it were, a little church, consecrated to Christ, and wholly influenced and governed by His rules.

Jonathan Edwards

— A Leader's Prayer —

Dear Lord, I am blessed to be part of the family of God where I find love and acceptance. You have also blessed me with my earthly family. Let me show love and acceptance for my own family so that through me, they might come to know You. Amen

Be strong and courageous, and do the work. Do not be afraid or discouraged, for the Lord God, my God, is with you.

1 Chronicles 28:20 NIV

BEYOND THE FEAR OF FAILURE

As we consider the uncertainties of the future, we are confronted with a powerful temptation: the temptation to "play it safe." Unwilling to move mountains, we fret over molehills. Unwilling to entertain great hopes for the tomorrow, we focus on the unfairness of the today. Unwilling to trust God completely, we take timid half-steps when God intends that we make giant leaps.

Today, ask God for the courage to step beyond the boundaries of your doubts. Ask Him to guide you to a place where you can realize your full potential—a place where you are freed from the fear of failure. Ask Him to do His part, and promise Him that you will do your part. Don't ask Him to lead you to a "safe" place; ask Him to lead you to the "right" place . . . and remember: those two places are seldom the same.

— A LEADERSHIP TIP —

If you're too afraid of failure, you may not live up to your potential. Remember that failing isn't nearly as bad as failing to try.

There comes a time when we simply have to face the challenges in our lives and stop backing down.

John Eldredge

With each new experience of letting God be in control, we gain courage and reinforcement for daring to do it again and again.

Gloria Gaither

Risk must be taken because the greatest hazard in life is to risk nothing.

John Maxwell

Do not be one of those who, rather than risk failure, never attempt anything.

Thomas Merton

Only a person who dares to risk is free.

Joey Johnson

— A Leader's Prayer —

Dear Lord, even when I'm afraid of failure, give me the courage to try. Remind me that with You by my side, I really have nothing to fear. So today, Father, I will live courageously as I place my faith in You. Amen

VERSE 30

The fear of the Lord is the beginning of wisdom, and the knowledge of the Holy One is understanding.

Proverbs 9:10 HCSB

WISE LEADERS FEAR GOD

Do you have a healthy, fearful respect for God's power? If so, you are both wise and obedient. And, because you are a thoughtful believer, you also understand that genuine wisdom begins with a profound appreciation for God's limitless power.

God praises humility and punishes pride. That's why God's greatest servants will always be those humble men and women who care less for their own glory and more for God's glory. In God's kingdom, the only way to achieve greatness is to shun it. And the only way to be wise is to understand these facts: God is great; He is all-knowing; and He is all-powerful. We must respect Him, and we must humbly obey His commandments, or we must accept the consequences of our misplaced pride.

— A LEADERSHIP TIP —

Your respect for God should make you fearful of disobeying Him . . . very fearful.

The remarkable thing about fearing God is that when you fear God, you fear nothing else, whereas if you do not fear God, you fear everything else.

Oswald Chambers

If we do not tremble before God, the world's system seems wonderful to us and pleasantly consumes us.

James Montgomery Boice

A healthy fear of God will do much to deter us from sin.

Charles Swindoll

It is not possible that mortal men should be thoroughly conscious of the divine presence without being filled with awe.

C. H. Spurgeon

When true believers are awed by the greatness of God and by the privilege of becoming His children, then they become sincerely motivated, effective evangelists.

Bill Hybels

— A LEADER'S PRAYER —

Dear Lord, let my greatest fear be the fear of displeasing You. I will strive, Father, to obey Your commandments and seek Your will this day and every day of my life. Amen

Let us lay aside every weight and the sin that so easily ensnares us, and run with endurance the race that lies before us, keeping our eyes on Jesus, the source and perfecter of our faith.

Hebrews 12:1-2 HCSB

THE RIGHT FOCUS

What is your focus today? Are you willing to focus your thoughts and energies on God's blessings and upon His will for your life? Or will you turn your thoughts to other things? Before you answer that question, consider this: God created you in His own image, and He wants you to experience joy and abundance. But, God will not force His joy upon you; you must claim it for yourself.

This day—and every day hereafter—is a chance to celebrate the life and the leadership opportunities that God has given you. It's also a chance to give thanks to the One who has offered you more blessings than you can possibly count.

Today, why not focus your thoughts on the joy that is rightfully yours in Christ? Why not take time to celebrate God's glorious creation? Why not trust your hopes instead of your fears? When you do, you will think optimistically about yourself and your world . . . and you can then share your optimism with others. They'll be better for it, and so will you.

— A Leadership Tip —

No steam or river ever drives anything until it is confined. No Niagara is ever turned into light and power until it is harnessed. No life ever grows until it is focused, dedicated, disciplined.

Harry Emerson Fosdick

For purposes of action nothing is more useful than narrowness of thought combined with energy of will.

Henri Frédéric Amiel

You can have anything you want—if you want it badly enough. You can be anything you want to be and you can do anything you set out to accomplish if you hold to that desire with singleness of purpose.

Abraham Lincoln

Don't let worry rob you of the joy that is rightfully yours. God is in heaven, and He knows your every need. Focus on God and His provisions, and watch gratefully as the worries of today begin to fade away.

Marie T. Freeman

— A Leader's Prayer —

Dear Lord, help me to face this day with a spirit of optimism and thanksgiving. And let me focus my thoughts on You and Your incomparable gifts. Amen

Then He said to them all, "If anyone desires to come after Me, let him deny himself, and take up his cross daily, and follow Me. For whoever desires to save his life will lose it, but whoever loses his life for My sake will save it."

Luke 9:23-24 NKJV

FOLLOW HIM

Jesus walks with you. Are you walking with Him? Hopefully, you will choose to walk with Him today and every day of your life.

Jesus loved you so much that He endured unspeakable humiliation and suffering for you. How will you respond to Christ's sacrifice? Will you follow the instructions of Luke 9:23 by taking up His cross and following Him? Or will you choose another path? When you place your hopes squarely at the foot of the cross, when you place Jesus squarely at the center of your life, you will be blessed. If you seek to be a worthy disciple of Jesus, you must acknowledge that He never comes "next." He is always first.

Do you hope to fulfill God's purpose for your life? Do you seek a life of abundance and peace? Do you intend to be Christian, not just in name, but in deed? Then follow Christ. Follow Him by picking up His cross today and every day that you live. When you do, you will quickly discover that Christ's love has the power to change everything, including you.

— A Leadership Tip —

Christ-centered leadership isn't easy. It takes a radical commitment—and significant sacrifices—to really follow Jesus. And it's worth it.

We have in Jesus Christ a perfect example of how to put God's truth into practice.

Bill Bright

As we live moment by moment under the control of the Spirit, His character, which is the character of Jesus, becomes evident to those around us.

Anne Graham Lotz

Our battles are first won or lost in the secret places of our will in God's presence, never in full view of the world.

Oswald Chambers

— A Leader's Prayer —

Dear Jesus, My life has been changed forever by Your love and sacrifice. Today I will praise You, I will honor You, and I will walk with You. Amen

For I know the thoughts that I think toward you, says the Lord, thoughts of peace and not of evil, to give you a future and a hope. Then you will call upon Me and go and pray to Me, and I will listen to you.

Jeremiah 29:11-12 NKJV

YOUR VERY BRIGHT FUTURE

Because we are saved by a risen Christ, we can have hope for the future, no matter how troublesome our present circumstances may seem. After all, God has promised that we are His throughout eternity. And, He has told us that we must place our hopes in Him.

Of course, we will face disappointments and failures while we are here on earth, but these are only temporary defeats. This world can be a place of trials and tribulations, but when we place our trust in the Giver of all things good, we are secure. God has promised us peace, joy, and eternal life. And God keeps His promises today, tomorrow, and forever.

Are you willing to place your future in the hands of a loving and all-knowing God? Do you trust in the ultimate goodness of His plan for your life? Will you face today's challenges with optimism and hope? You should. After all, God created you for a very important purpose: His purpose. And you still have important work to do: His work.

Today, as you live in the present and look to the future, remember that God has a plan for you. Act—and believe—accordingly.

— A Leadership Tip —

Even when the world seems dark, the future is bright for those who look to the Son.

Every experience God gives us, every person he brings into our lives, is the perfect preparation for the future that only he can see.

Corrie ten Boom

The future lies all before us. Shall it only be a slight advance upon what we usually do? Ought it not to be a bound, a leap forward to altitudes of endeavor and success undreamed of before?

Annie Armstrong

Take courage. We walk in the wilderness today and in the Promised Land tomorrow.

D. L. Moody

— A Leader's Prayer —

Dear Lord, my hope is in You. Give me the courage to face the future with certainty, and give me the wisdom to follow in the footsteps of Your Son, today and forever. Amen

But this I say: He who sows sparingly will also reap sparingly, and he who sows bountifully will also reap bountifully. So let each one give as he purposes in his heart, not grudgingly or of necessity; for God loves a cheerful giver.

2 Corinthians 9:6-7 NKJV

WISE LEADERS ARE GENEROUS

The thread of generosity is woven—completely and inextricably—into the very fabric of Christ's teachings. As He sent His disciples out to heal the sick and spread God's message of salvation, Jesus offered this guiding principle: "Freely you have received, freely give" (Matthew 10:8 NIV). The principle still applies. If we are to be disciples of Christ, we must give freely of our time, our possessions, and our love.

In 2 Corinthians 9, Paul reminds us that when we sow the seeds of generosity, we reap bountiful rewards in accordance with God's plan for our lives. Thus, we are instructed to give cheerfully and without reservation. So today, make this pledge and keep it: Be a cheerful, generous, courageous giver. The world needs your help, and you need the spiritual rewards that will be yours when you give it.

— A Leadership Tip —

God has given so much to you, and He wants you to share His gifts with others.

We are never more like God than when we give.

Charles Swindoll

God does not need our money. But, you and I need the experience of giving it.

James Dobson

The happiest and most joyful people are those who give money and serve.

Dave Ramsey

Abundant living means abundant giving.

E. Stanley Jones

God does not supply money to satisfy our every whim and desire. His promise is to meet our needs and provide an abundance so that we can help other people.

Larry Burkett

— A Leader's Prayer —

Lord, You have given me so much. Let me share my blessings with those in need. Make me a generous, humble Christian leader, Lord, and let the glory be Yours and Yours alone. Amen

75

You shall have no other gods before Me.

Exodus 20:3 NKJV

WISE LEADERS PUT GOD FIRST

Is God your top priority? Have you given His Son your heart, your soul, your talents, and your time? Or are you in the habit of giving God little more than a few hours on Sunday morning? The answers to these questions will determine the direction of your life and the quality of your leadership.

As you contemplate your own relationship with God, remember this: all of mankind is engaged in the practice of worship. Some people choose to worship God and, as a result, reap the joy that He intends for His children. Others distance themselves from God by worshiping such things as earthly possessions or personal gratification . . . and when they do so, they suffer.

In the book of Exodus, God warns that we should place no gods before Him. Yet all too often, we place our Lord in second place as we worship the gods of pride, greed, power, or lust.

When we place our desires for material possessions above our love for God—or when we yield to temptations of the flesh—we find ourselves engaged in a struggle that is similar to the one Jesus faced when He was tempted by Satan. In the wilderness,

Satan offered Jesus earthly power and unimaginable riches, but Jesus turned Satan away and chose instead to worship God. We must do likewise by putting God first and worshiping only Him.

Does God rule your heart? Make certain that the honest answer to this question is a resounding yes. In the life of every righteous believer, God comes first. And that's precisely the place that He deserves in your heart, too.

— A Leadership Tip —

As you establish priorities for your day and your life, God deserves first place. And you deserve the experience of putting Him there.

Jesus Christ is the first and last, author and finisher, beginning and end, alpha and omega, and by Him all other things hold together. He must be first or nothing. God never comes next!

Vance Havner

— A Leader's Prayer —

Dear Lord, keep me mindful of the need to place You first in every aspect of my life. You have blessed me beyond measure, Father, and I will praise You with my thoughts, my prayers, my testimony, and my service, this day and every day. Amen

In all your ways acknowledge Him, and He shall direct your paths.

Proverbs 3:6 NKJV

WISE LEADERS SEEK GOD'S GUIDANCE

When we genuinely seek to know the heart of God—when we prayerfully seek His wisdom and His will—our Heavenly Father carefully guides us over the peaks and valleys of life. And as Christians, we can be comforted: Whether we find ourselves at the pinnacle of the mountain or the darkest depths of the valley, the loving heart of God is always there with us.

As Christians whose salvation has been purchased by the blood of Christ, we have every reason to live—and to lead—courageously. After all, Christ has already fought and won our battle for us—He did so on the cross at Calvary. But despite Christ's sacrifice, and despite God's promises, we may become confused or disoriented by the endless complications and countless distractions of life.

If you're unsure of your next step, lean upon God's promises and lift your prayers to Him. Remember that God is always near; remember that He is your protector and your deliverer. Open yourself to His heart, and trust Him to guide your path. When you do, God will direct your steps, and you will receive His blessings today, tomorrow, and throughout eternity.

— A Leadership Tip —

If you want God's guidance, ask for it. When you pray for guidance, God will give it.

Enjoy the adventure of receiving God's guidance. Taste it, revel in it, appreciate the fact that the journey is often a lot more exciting than arriving at the destination.

Bill Hybels

Walk in the daylight of God's will because then you will be safe; you will not stumble.

Anne Graham Lotz

It is a joy that God never abandons His children. He guides faithfully all who listen to His directions.

Corrie ten Boom

— A Leader's Prayer —

Today, Lord, let me count my blessings with thanksgiving in my heart. You have cared for me, Lord, and I will give You the glory and the praise. Let me accept Your blessings and Your gifts, and let me share them with others, just as You first shared them with me. Amen

Good leadership is a channel of water controlled by God; he directs it to whatever ends he chooses.

Proverbs 21:1 MSG

WISE LEADERS SEEK GOD'S SUPPORT

It is easy to become overwhelmed by the demands of everyday life, but if you're a faithful follower of the One from Galilee, you need never be overwhelmed. Why? Because God's love is sufficient to meet your needs. Whatever dangers you may face, whatever heartbreaks you must endure, God is with you, and He stands ready to comfort you and to heal you.

The Psalmist writes, "Weeping may endure for a night, but joy comes in the morning" (Psalm 30:5 NKJV). But when we are suffering, the morning may seem very far away. It is not. God promises that He is "near to those who have a broken heart" (Psalm 34:18 NKJV).

If you are experiencing the intense pain of a recent loss, or if you are still mourning a loss from long ago, perhaps you are now ready to begin the next stage of your journey with God. If so, be mindful of this fact: the loving heart of God is sufficient to meet any challenge, including yours.

— A Leadership Tip —

Whatever you need, God can provide. He is always sufficient to meet your needs.

We shall find in Christ enough of everything we need—for the body, for the mind, and for the spirit—to do what He wants us to do as long as He wants us to do it.

Vance Havner

God's help is near and always available, but it is only given to those who seek it.

Max Lucado

How delightful a teacher, but gentle a provider, how bountiful a giver is my Father! Praise, praise to Thee, O manifested Most High.

Jim Elliot

— A Leader's Prayer —

Dear Lord, today I come to You seeking guidance. I will trust You to show me the path that I should take, and I will strive, as best I can, to follow in the footsteps of Your Son. Amen

Unless the Lord builds a house, its builders labor over it in vain; unless the Lord watches over a city, the watchman stays alert in vain.

Psalm 127:1 HSCB

WISE LEADERS KNOW THAT GOD PROTECTS HIS CHILDREN

Have you ever faced leadership challenges that seemed too big to handle? Have you ever faced big problems that, despite your best efforts, simply could not be solved? If so, you know how uncomfortable it is to feel helpless in the face of difficult circumstances. Thankfully, even when there's nowhere else to turn, you can turn your thoughts and prayers to God, and He will respond.

God's hand uplifts those who turn their hearts and prayers to Him. Count yourself among that number. When you do, you can live courageously and joyfully, knowing that "this too will pass"—but that God's love for you will not. And you can draw strength from the knowledge that you are a marvelous creation, loved, protected, and uplifted by the ever-present hand of God.

— A LEADERSHIP TIP —
When you are in the center of God's will, you are in the center of God's protection.

When you fall and skin your knees and skin your heart, He'll pick you up.

Charles Stanley

My case is urgent, and I do not see how I am to be delivered; but this is no business of mine. He who makes the promise will find ways and means of keeping it. It is mine to obey His command; it is not mine to direct His counsels. I am His servant, not His solicitor. I call upon Him, and He will deliver.

C. H. Spurgeon

Trials are not enemies of faith but opportunities to reveal God's faithfulness.

Barbara Johnson

There is no safer place to live than the center of His will.

Calvin Miller

— A Leader's Prayer —

Dear Lord, You have blessed me with so much: Your love, Your mercy, and Your grace. Enable me to be merciful toward others, Father, just as You have been merciful toward me so that I might share Your love with all who cross my path. Amen

The Lord is my shepherd; I shall not want. He makes me to lie down in green pastures; He leads me beside the still waters. He restores my soul.

Psalm 23:1-3 NKJV

WISE LEADERS KNOW THAT GOD IS THEIR SHEPHERD

David, the author of the 23rd Psalm, realized that God was his shield, his protector, and his salvation. And if we're wise, we realize it, too. After all, God has promised to protect us, and He intends to keep His promise.

In a world filled with dangers and temptations, God is the ultimate armor. In a world filled with misleading messages, God's Word is the ultimate truth. In a world filled with more frustrations than we can count, God's Son offers the ultimate peace.

Will you accept God's peace and wear God's armor against the dangers of our world? Hopefully so—because when you do, you can live courageously, knowing that you possess the supreme protection: God's unfailing love for you.

The world offers no safety nets, but God does. He sent His only begotten Son to offer you the priceless gift of eternal life. And now you are challenged to return God's love by obeying His commandments and honoring His Son.

Sometimes, in the crush of everyday life, God may seem far away, but He is not. God is everywhere you have ever been and everywhere you will ever go. He is with you night and day; He knows your thoughts and your prayers. And, when you earnestly seek His protection, you will find it because He is here—always—waiting patiently for you to reach out to Him. And the next move, of course, is yours.

— A LEADERSHIP TIP —

Earthly security is an illusion. Your only real security comes from the loving heart of God.

God does not promise to keep us out of the storms and floods, but He does promise to sustain us in the storm, and then bring us out in due time for His glory when the storm has done its work.

Warren Wiersbe

Kept by His power—that is the only safety.

Oswald Chambers

— A LEADER'S PRAYER —

Dear Lord, I will earnestly seek Your will for my life. You have a plan for me that I can never fully understand. But You understand. And I will trust You today, tomorrow, and forever. Amen

Cast thy burden upon the LORD, and he shall sustain thee: he shall never suffer the righteous to be moved.

Psalm 55:22 KJV

WHERE TO PLACE YOUR BURDENS

God's Word contains promises upon which we, as Christians, can and must depend. The Bible is a priceless gift, a tool that God intends for us to use in every aspect of our lives. Too many Christians, however, keep their spiritual tool kits tightly closed and out of sight.

Psalm 55:22 instructs us to cast our burdens upon the Lord. And that's perfect advice for men, women, and children alike.

Are you tired? Discouraged? Fearful? Be comforted and trust the promises that God has made to you. Are you worried or anxious? Be confident in God's power. He will never desert you. Do you see a difficult future ahead? Be courageous and call upon God. He will protect you and then use you according to His purposes. Are you confused? Listen to the quiet voice of your Heavenly Father. He is not a God of confusion. Talk with Him; listen to Him; trust Him, and trust His promises. He is steadfast, and He is your Protector . . . forever.

— A LEADERSHIP TIP —

God is big enough to handle your challenges. Corrie ten Boom advised, "God's all-sufficiency is a major. Your inability is a minor. Major in majors, not in minors." Enough said.

Faith is not merely you holding on to God—it is God holding on to you.

E. Stanley Jones

Measure the size of the obstacles against the size of God.

Beth Moore

God wants to reveal Himself as your heavenly Father. When you are hurting, you can run to Him and crawl up into His lap. When you wonder which way to turn, you can grasp His strong hand, and He'll guide you along life's path. When everything around you is falling apart, you'll feel your Father's arm around your shoulder to hold you together.

Lisa Whelchel

— A LEADER'S PRAYER —

Dear Lord, as I face the challenges of this day, You will protect me. I thank You, Father, for Your love and for Your strength. I will lean upon You today and forever. Amen

To everything there is a season, a time for every purpose under heaven

Ecclesiastes 3:1 NKJV

WISE LEADERS TRUST GOD'S TIMING

Sometimes, the hardest thing to do is to wait. This is especially true when we're in a hurry and when we want things to happen now, if not sooner! But God's plan does not always happen in the way that we would like or at the time of our own choosing. Our task—as thoughtful men and women who trust in a benevolent, all-knowing Father—is to wait patiently for God to reveal Himself.

We humans know precisely what we want, and we know exactly when we want it. But, God has a far better plan for each of us. He has created a world that unfolds according to His own timetable, not ours . . . thank goodness! And if we're wise, we trust Him and we wait patiently for Him. After all, He is trustworthy, and He always knows best.

— A LEADERSHIP TIP —

You don't know precisely what you need—or when you need it—but God does. So trust His timing.

God does not promise to keep us out of the storms and floods, but He does promise to sustain us in the storm, and then bring us out in due time for His glory when the storm has done its work.

Warren Wiersbe

When our plans are interrupted, his are not. His plans are proceeding exactly as scheduled, moving us always—including those minutes or hours or years which seem most useless or wasted or unendurable—toward the goal of true maturity.

Elisabeth Elliot

Your times are in His hands. He's in charge of the timetable, so wait patiently.

Kay Arthur

God's delays and His ways can be confusing because the process God uses to accomplish His will can go against human logic and common sense.

Anne Graham Lotz

— A Leader's Prayer —

Dear Lord, Your wisdom is infinite, and the timing of Your Heavenly plan is perfect. You have a plan for my life that is grander than I can imagine. When I am impatient, remind me that You are never early or late. You are always on time, Father, so let me trust in You. Amen

All Scripture is given by inspiration of God, and is profitable for doctrine, for reproof, for correction, for instruction in righteousness, that the man of God may be complete, thoroughly equipped for every good work.

2 Timothy 3:16-17 NKJV

WISE LEADERS DEPEND UPON SCRIPTURE

Is Bible study a high priority for you? The answer to this simple question will determine, to a surprising extent, the quality of your life and the direction of your faith.

As you establish priorities for life, you must decide whether God's Word will be a bright spotlight that guides your path every day or a tiny nightlight that occasionally flickers in the dark. The decision to study the Bible—or not—is yours and yours alone. But make no mistake: how you choose to use your Bible will have a profound impact on you and your loved ones.

George Mueller observed, "The vigor of our spiritual lives will be in exact proportion to the place held by the Bible in our lives and in our thoughts." Think of it like this: the more you use your Bible, the more God will use you.

Perhaps you're one of those Christians who owns a bookshelf full of unread Bibles. If so, remember the old saying, "A Bible in the hand is worth two in the bookcase." Or perhaps you're one of those folks who is simply "too busy" to find time for a daily dose of prayer and Bible study. If so, remember the old adage, "It's hard to stumble when you're on your knees."

God's Word can be a roadmap to a place of righteousness and abundance. Make it your roadmap. God's wisdom can be a light to guide your steps. Claim it as your light today, tomorrow, and every day of your life—and then walk confidently in the footsteps of God's only begotten Son.

— A Leadership Tip —

God intends for you to use His Word as your guidebook for life and for leadership. Your intentions should be the same.

My meditation and study have shown me that, like God, His Word is holy, everlasting, absolutely true, powerful, personally fair, and never changing.

Bill Bright

— A Leader's Prayer —

Heavenly Father, Your Holy Word is a light unto the world; let me study it, trust it, and share it with all who cross my path. In all that I do, help me be a worthy witness for You as I share the Good News of Your perfect Son and Your perfect Word. Amen

Therefore, whatever you want others to do for you, do also the same for them—this is the Law and the Prophets.

Matthew 7:12 HCSB

GREAT LEADERS OBEY THE GOLDEN RULE

The words of Matthew 7:12 remind us that, as believers in Christ, we are commanded to treat others as we wish to be treated. This commandment is, indeed, the Golden Rule for Christians of every generation. When we weave the thread of kindness into the very fabric of our lives, we give glory to the One who gave His life for ours.

Because we are imperfect human beings, we are, on occasion, selfish, thoughtless, or cruel. But God commands us to behave otherwise. He teaches us to rise above our own imperfections and to treat others with unselfishness and love. When we observe God's Golden Rule, we help build His kingdom here on earth. And, when we share the love of Christ, we share a priceless gift; may we share it today and every day that we live.

— A LEADERSHIP TIP —
When in doubt, be a little kinder than necessary.

The golden rule to follow to obtain spiritual understanding is not one of intellectual pursuit, but one of obedience.

Oswald Chambers

Faith never asks whether good works are to be done, but has done them before there is time to ask the question, and it is always doing them.

Martin Luther

Love is not grabbing, or self-centered, or selfish. Real love is being able to contribute to the happiness of another person without expecting to get anything in return.

James Dobson

Find out how much God has given you and from it take what you need; the remainder is needed by others.

St. Augustine

— A Leader's Prayer —

Dear Lord, let me treat others as I wish to be treated. Because I expect kindness, let me be kind. Because I wish to be loved, let me be loving. Because I need forgiveness, let me be merciful. In all things, Lord, let me live by the Golden Rule that is the commandment of Your Son Jesus. Amen

Whoever conceals an offense promotes love, but whoever gossips about it separates friends.

Proverbs 17:9 HCSB

WISE LEADERS DON'T GOSSIP

The Bible clearly tells us that gossip is wrong. But when it comes to the special confidences that you share with your very closest friends, gossip can be disastrous.

The Bible reminds us that "Reckless words pierce like a sword, but the tongue of the wise brings healing" (Proverbs 12:18 NIV). Therefore, if we are to solve more problems than we start, we must measure our words carefully, and we must never betray a confidence. But sometimes even the most thoughtful among us may speak first and think second (with decidedly mixed results).

When we speak too quickly, we may say things that would be better left unsaid. When we forgo the wonderful opportunity to consider our thoughts before we give voice to them, we're putting ourselves and our relationships in danger.

A far better strategy, of course, is to do the more difficult thing: to think first and to speak next. When we do so, we give ourselves ample time to compose our thoughts and to consult our Creator before we say something that we might soon regret.

— A LEADERSHIP TIP —

When talking about other people, use this guideline: don't say something behind someone's back that you wouldn't say to that person directly.

Dismiss all anger and look into yourself a little. Remember that he of whom you are speaking is your brother and, as he is in the way of salvation, God can make him a saint, in spite of his present weakness.

St. Thomas of Villanova

Go to church to pray, not gossip.

St. Boniface of Mainz

We should have great peace if we did not busy ourselves with what others say and do.

Thomas à Kempis

A little kindly advice is better than a great deal of scolding.

Fanny Crosby

— A LEADER'S PRAYER —

Dear Lord, it's tempting to gossip, but it's wrong. Today and every day, help me speak words that are pleasing to You, and help me treat other people in the same way that I want to be treated by them. Amen

*Rejoice always, pray without ceasing, in everything give
thanks; for this is the will of God in Christ Jesus for you.*

1 Thessalonians 5:16-18 NKJV

WISE LEADERS ARE GRATEFUL

For most of us, life is busy and complicated. We
have countless responsibilities, some of which begin before sunrise and many of which end long after
sunset. Amid the rush and crush of the daily grind,
it is easy to lose sight of God and His blessings. But,
when we forget to slow down and say "Thank You"
to our Maker, we rob ourselves of His presence, His
peace, and His joy.

Your task, as a Christian leader, is to praise God
many times each day. Then, with gratitude in your
heart, you can face your daily duties with the perspective and power that only He can provide.

— A LEADERSHIP TIP —

Developing an attitude of gratitude is key to a joyful and satisfying life. So ask yourself this question:
"Am I grateful enough?"

Reflect upon your present blessings, of which every man has many—not on your past misfortunes, of which all men have some.

Charles Dickens

We become happy, spiritually prosperous people not because we receive what we want, but because we appreciate what we have.

Penelope Stokes

Contentment comes when we develop an attitude of gratitude for the important things we do have in our lives that we tend to take for granted if we have our eyes staring longingly at our neighbor's stuff.

Dave Ramsey

It is only with gratitude that life becomes rich.

Dietrich Bonhoeffer

If you won't fill your heart with gratitude, the devil will fill it with something else.

Marie T. Freeman

— A Leader's Prayer —

Dear Lord, You have given me much; when I think of Your grace and goodness, I am humbled and thankful. Today, I will praise You, not just through my words, but also through my deeds. Let the words that I speak and the actions that I take bring honor to You and to Your Son. Amen

Go, therefore, and make disciples of all nations, baptizing them in the name of the Father and of the Son and of the Holy Spirit, teaching them to observe everything I have commanded you. And remember, I am with you always, to the end of the age.

Matthew 28:19-20 HCSB

THE GREAT COMMISSION

Are you a bashful Christian, one who is afraid to speak up for your Savior? Do you leave it up to others to share their testimonies while you stand on the sidelines, reluctant to share yours? Too many of us are slow to obey the last commandment of the risen Christ; we don't do our best to "make disciples of all the nations."

Christ's Great Commission applies to Christians of every generation, including our own. As believers, we are commanded to share the Good News with our families, with our neighbors, and with the world. Jesus invited His disciples to become fishers of men. We, too, must accept the Savior's invitation, and we must do so today. Tomorrow may indeed be too late.

— A LEADERSHIP TIP —

The best day to respond to Christ's Great Commission is this day.

You cannot keep silent once you have experienced salvation of Jesus Christ.

Warren Wiersbe

Our commission is quite specific. We are told to be His witness to all nations. For us, as His disciples, to refuse any part of this commission frustrates the love of Jesus Christ, the Son of God.

Catherine Marshall

There are many timid souls whom we jostle morning and evening as we pass them by; but if only the kind word were spoken they might become fully persuaded.

Fanny Crosby

Your light is the truth of the Gospel message itself as well as your witness as to Who Jesus is and what He has done for you. Don't hide it.

Anne Graham Lotz

— A Leader's Prayer —

Dear Lord, let me share the Good News of Your Son Jesus. Let the life that I live and the words that I speak be a witness to my faith in Him. And let me share the story of my salvation with others so that they, too, might receive His eternal gifts. Amen

Guard your heart above all else, for it is the source of life.

Proverbs 4:23 HCSB

WISE LEADERS UNDERSTAND THAT HABITS MATTER

It's an old saying and a true one: First, you make your habits, and then your habits make you. Some habits will inevitably bring you closer to God; other habits will lead you away from the path He has chosen for you. If you sincerely desire to improve your spiritual health, you must honestly examine the habits that make up the fabric of your day. And you must abandon those habits that are displeasing to God.

If you trust God, and if you keep asking for His help, He can transform your life. If you sincerely ask Him to help you, the same God who created the universe will help you defeat the harmful habits that have heretofore defeated you. So, if at first you don't succeed, keep praying. God is listening, and He's ready to help you become a better person if you ask Him . . . so ask today.

— A LEADERSHIP TIP —

Since behaviors become habits, make them work with you and not against you.

E. Stanley Jones

You will never change your life until you change something you do daily.

John Maxwell

You can build up a set of good habits so that you habitually take the Christian way without thought.

E. Stanley Jones

Begin to be now what you will be hereafter.

St. Jerome

If you want to form a new habit, get to work. If you want to break a bad habit, get on your knees.

Marie T. Freeman

— A Leader's Prayer —

Dear Lord, help me break bad habits and form good ones. And let my actions be pleasing to You, today, tomorrow, and every day of my life. Amen

Carry one another's burdens; in this way you will fulfill the law of Christ.

Galatians 6:2 HCSB

WISE LEADERS ARE HELPFUL

Neighbors, friends, and coworkers. We know that we are instructed to love them, and yet there's so little time . . . and we're so busy. No matter. As Christians, we are commanded by our Lord and Savior Jesus Christ to love our neighbors just as we love ourselves. We are not asked to love our neighbors, nor are we encouraged to do so. We are commanded to love them. Period.

In order to love our neighbors as God intends, we must first slow down long enough to understand their needs. Slowing down, however, is not as simple as it seems. We live in a fast-paced world with pressures and demands that often sap our time and our energy. Sometimes, we may convince ourselves that slowing down is not an option, but we are wrong. Caring for our neighbors must be our priority because it is God's priority.

This very day, perhaps at your church or workplace, you will encounter someone who needs a word of encouragement, or a pat on the back, or a helping hand, or a heartfelt prayer. And, if you don't reach out, who will? If you don't take the time to understand the needs of your associates, who will? If you don't love your brothers and sisters, who will? So, today, look for a person in need . . . and then do something to help. Father's orders.

— A LEADERSHIP TIP —

Start each day by asking this question: "Who can I help today?"

Encouraging others means helping people, looking for the best in them, and trying to bring out their positive qualities.

John Maxwell

Do all the good you can. By all the means you can. In all the ways you can. In all the places you can. At all the times you can. To all the people you can. As long as ever you can.

John Wesley

— A LEADER'S PRAYER —

Dear Lord, let me help others in every way that I can. Jesus served others; I can too. I will serve other people with my good deeds and with my prayers, today and every day. Amen

Let us hold on to the confession of our hope without wavering, for He who promised is faithful.

Hebrews 10:23 HCSB

WISE LEADERS ARE ALWAYS HOPEFUL

Despite God's promises, despite Christ's love, and despite our countless blessings, we frail human beings can still lose hope from time to time. When we do, we need the encouragement of Christian friends, the life-changing power of prayer, and the healing truth of God's Holy Word.

If you find yourself falling into the spiritual traps of worry and discouragement, seek the healing touch of Jesus and the encouraging words of fellow Christians. And remember the words of our Savior: "These things I have spoken unto you, that in me ye might have peace. In the world ye shall have tribulation: but be of good cheer; I have overcome the world" (John 16:33 KJV). This world can be a place of trials and tribulations, but as believers, we are secure. God has promised us peace, joy, and eternal life. And, of course, God keeps His promises today, tomorrow, and forever.

— A LEADERSHIP TIP —

If you're experiencing hard times, you'll be wise to start spending more time with God. And if you do your part, God will do His part. So never be afraid to hope—or to ask—for a miracle.

Hope is faith holding out its hand in the dark.

Barbara Johnson

Troubles we bear trustfully can bring us a fresh vision of God and a new outlook on life, an outlook of peace and hope.

Billy Graham

I discovered that sorrow was not to be feared but rather endured with hope and expectancy that God would use it to visit and bless my life.

Jill Briscoe

— A LEADER'S PRAYER —

Today, Dear Lord, I will live in hope. If I become discouraged, I will turn to You. If I grow weary, I will seek strength in You. In every aspect of my life, I will trust You. You are my Father, Lord, and I place my hope and my faith in You. Amen

The greatest among you must be a servant. But those who exalt themselves will be humbled, and those who humble themselves will be exalted.

Matthew 23:11-12 NKJV

WISE LEADERS UNDERSTAND THAT IT'S IMPORTANT TO BE HUMBLE

As fallible human beings, we have so much to be humble about. Why, then, is humility such a difficult trait for us to master? Precisely because we are fallible human beings. Yet if we are to grow and mature as Christians, we must strive to give credit where credit is due, starting, of course, with God and His only begotten Son.

As Christians, we have been refashioned and saved by Jesus Christ, and that salvation came not because of our own good works but because of God's grace. Thus, we are not "self-made"; we are "God-made" and we are "Christ-saved." How, then, can we be boastful? The answer, of course, is that, if we are honest with ourselves and with our God, we simply can't be boastful . . . we must, instead, be eternally grateful and exceedingly humble. Humility, however, is not easy for most of us. All too often, we are tempted to stick out our chests and say, "Look at me; look what I did!" But, in the quiet moments when we search the depths of our own hearts, we know better. Whatever "it" is, God did that. And He deserves the credit.

— A LEADERSHIP TIP —

As a leader, you must remain humble or face the consequences. Pride does go before the fall, but humility often prevents the fall.

If you know who you are in Christ, your personal ego is not an issue.

Beth Moore

Because Christ Jesus came to the world clothed in humility, he will always be found among those who are clothed with humility. He will be found among the humble people.

A. W. Tozer

— A LEADER'S PRAYER —

Heavenly Father, Jesus clothed Himself with humility when He chose to leave heaven and come to earth to live and die for us, His children. Christ is my Master and my example. Clothe me with humility, Lord, so that I might be more like Your Son, and keep me mindful that You are the giver and sustainer of life, and to You, Dear Lord, goes the glory and the praise. Amen

VERSE 51

An overseer, therefore, must be above reproach, the husband of one wife, self-controlled, sensible, respectable, hospitable, an able teacher, not addicted to wine, not a bully but gentle, not quarrelsome, not greedy.

1 Timothy 3:2-3 HCSB

WISE LEADERS UNDERSTAND THAT INTEGRITY MATTERS

Integrity is built slowly over a lifetime. It is the sum of every right decision and every honest word. It is forged on the anvil of honorable work and polished by the twin virtues of honesty and fairness. Integrity is a precious thing—difficult to build but easy to tear down.

As believers in Christ, we must seek to live each day with discipline, honesty, and faith. When we do, at least two things happen: integrity becomes a habit, and God blesses us because of our obedience to Him.

Living a life of integrity isn't always the easiest way, but it is always the right way. God clearly intends that it should be our way, too.

It has been said that character is what we are when nobody is watching. How true. When we do things that we know aren't right, we try to hide them from our families and friends. But even if we successfully conceal our sins from the world, we can never conceal our sins from God.

If you sincerely wish to walk with your Creator, follow His commandments. When you do, your character will take care of itself . . . and you won't need to look over your shoulder to see who, besides God, is watching.

— A LEADERSHIP TIP —

Integrity pays big dividends. Deception creates massive headaches. Behave accordingly.

Maintaining your integrity in a world of sham is no small accomplishment.

Wayne Oates

Integrity is the glue that holds our way of life together. We must constantly strive to keep our integrity intact. When wealth is lost, nothing is lost; when health is lost, something is lost; when character is lost, all is lost.

Billy Graham

— A LEADER'S PRAYER —

Heavenly Father, Your Word instructs me to walk in integrity and in truth. Make me a worthy leader, Lord. Let my words be true, and let my actions lead others to You. Amen

These things have I spoken unto you, that my joy might remain in you, and that your joy might be full.

John 15:11 KJV

MAKING HIS JOY YOUR JOY

Christ made it clear: He intends that His joy should become our joy. Yet sometimes, amid the inevitable hustle and bustle of life here on earth, we can forfeit—albeit temporarily—the joy of Christ as we wrestle with the challenges of daily living.

Jonathan Edwards, the 18th-century American clergyman, observed, "Christ is not only a remedy for your weariness and trouble, but he will give you an abundance of the contrary: joy and delight. They who come to Christ do not only come to a resting-place after they have been wandering in a wilderness, but they come to a banqueting-house where they may rest, and where they may feast. They may cease from their former troubles and toils, and they may enter upon a course of delights and spiritual joys."

If, today, your heart is heavy, open the door of your soul to Christ. He will give you peace and joy. And, if you already have the joy of Christ in your heart, share it freely, just as Christ freely shared His joy with you.

— A LEADERSHIP TIP —

Every day, God gives you many reasons to rejoice. The rest is up to you.

Joy is the direct result of having God's perspective on our daily lives and the effect of loving our Lord enough to obey His commands and trust His promises.

Bill Bright

If you can forgive the person you were, accept the person you are, and believe in the person you will become, you are headed for joy. So celebrate your life.

Barbara Johnson

The Christian lifestyle is not one of legalistic do's and don'ts, but one that is positive, attractive, and joyful.

Vonette Bright

— A LEADER'S PRAYER —

Dear Lord, You are my loving Heavenly Father, and You created me in Your image. As Your faithful child, I will make Your joy my joy. I will praise Your works, I will obey Your Word, and I will honor Your Son, this day and every day of my life. Amen

Do not judge, and you will not be judged. Do not condemn, and you will not be condemned. Forgive, and you will be forgiven.

Luke 6:37 HCSB

WISE LEADERS UNDERSTAND THE DANGER OF BEING JUDGMENTAL

We have all fallen short of God's commandments, and He has forgiven us. We, too, must forgive others. And, we must refrain from judging them.

Are you one of those people who finds it easy to judge others? If so, it's time to change.

God does not need (or, for that matter, want) your help. Why? Because God is perfectly capable of judging the human heart . . . while you are not.

As Christians, we are warned that to judge others is to invite fearful consequences: to the extent we judge others, so, too, will we be judged by God. Let us refrain, then, from judging our neighbors. Instead, let us forgive them and love them in the same way that God has forgiven us.

— A LEADERSHIP TIP —

When you catch yourself being overly judgmental, try to stop yourself and interrupt your critical thoughts before you become angry.

Judging draws the judgment of others.

Catherine Marshall

Christians think they are prosecuting attorneys or judges, when, in reality, God has called all of us to be witnesses.

Warren Wiersbe

Don't judge other people more harshly than you want God to judge you.

Marie T. Freeman

An individual Christian may see fit to give up all sorts of things for special reasons—marriage, or meat, or beer, or cinema; but the moment he starts saying these things are bad in themselves, or looking down his nose at other people who do use them, he has taken the wrong turn.

C. S. Lewis

— A LEADER'S PRAYER —

Dear Lord, sometimes I am quick to judge others. But, You have commanded me not to judge. Keep me mindful, Father, that when I judge others, I am living outside of Your will for my life. You have forgiven me, Lord. Let me forgive others, let me love them, and let me help them . . . without judging them. Amen

Assuredly, I say to you, inasmuch as you did it to one of the least of these My brethren, you did it to Me.

Matthew 25:40 NKJV

WISE LEADERS ARE KIND

In the busyness and confusion of daily life, it is easy to lose focus, and it is easy to become frustrated. We are imperfect human beings struggling to manage our lives as best we can, but we often fall short. When we are distracted or disappointed, we may neglect to share a kind word or a kind deed. This oversight hurts others, but it hurts us most of all.

Matthew 25:40 warns, "Inasmuch as you did it to one of the least of these My brethren, you did it to Me." When we extend the hand of friendship to those who need it most, God promises His blessings. When we ignore the needs of others—or mistreat them—we risk God's retribution.

Today, slow yourself down and be alert for those who need your smile, your kind words, or your helping hand. Make kindness a centerpiece of your dealings with others. They will be blessed, and you will be, too. When you spread a heaping helping of encouragement and hope to the world, you can't help getting a little bit on yourself.

— A LEADERSHIP TIP —

Kind words have echoes that last a lifetime and beyond.

When you extend hospitality to others, you're not trying to impress people, you're trying to reflect God to them.

Max Lucado

It is one of the most beautiful compensations of life that no one can sincerely try to help another without helping herself.

Barbara Johnson

Do all the good you can. By all the means you can. In all the ways you can. In all the places you can. At all the times you can. To all the people you can. As long as ever you can.

John Wesley

— A LEADER'S PRAYER —

Lord, make me a loving, encouraging Christian leader. And, let my love for Christ be reflected through the kindness that I show to my associates, to my family, to my friends, and to all who need the healing touch of the Master's hand. Amen

Shepherd God's flock among you, not overseeing out of compulsion but freely, according to God's will; not for the money but eagerly.

1 Peter 5:2 HCSB

CHRIST-CENTERED LEADERSHIP

The old saying is familiar and true: imitation is the sincerest form of flattery. As believers, we are called to imitate, as best we can, the carpenter from Galilee. The task of imitating Christ is often difficult and sometimes impossible, but as Christians, we must continue to try.

Our world needs leaders who willingly honor Christ with their words and their deeds, but not necessarily in that order. If you seek to be such a leader, then you must begin by making yourself a worthy example to your family, to your friends, to your church, and to your community. After all, your words of instruction will never ring true unless you yourself are willing to follow them.

Christ-centered leadership is an exercise in service: service to God in heaven and service to His children here on earth. Christ willingly became a servant to His followers, and you must seek to do the same for yours.

Are you the kind of servant-leader whom you would want to follow? If so, congratulations: you are honoring your Savior by imitating Him. And that, of course, is the sincerest form of flattery.

— A LEADERSHIP TIP —

Our world needs all the good leaders it can get, so don't be afraid to take a leadership role . . . now.

You can never separate a leader's actions from his character.

John Maxwell

A man ought to live so that everybody knows he is a Christian, and most of all, his family ought to know.

D. L. Moody

A true and safe leader is likely to be one who has not desire to lead, but is forced into a position of leadership by inward pressure of the Holy Spirit and the press of external situation.

A. W. Tozer

— A LEADER'S PRAYER —

Heavenly Father, when I find myself in a position of leadership, let me follow Your teachings and obey Your commandments. Make me a person of integrity and wisdom, Lord, and make me a worthy example to those whom I serve. And, let me turn to You, Lord, for guidance and for strength in all that I say and do. Amen

Listen, my son, to your father's instruction and do not forsake your mother's teaching.

Proverbs 1:8 NIV

WISE LEADERS KEEP LEARNING

The best leaders never stop learning. And, when it comes to learning life's lessons, we can either do things the easy way or the hard way. The easy way can be summed up as follows: when God teaches us a lesson, we learn it . . . the first time! Unfortunately, too many of us learn much more slowly than that.

When we resist God's instruction, He continues to teach, whether we like it or not. Our challenge, then, is to discern God's lessons from the experiences of everyday life. Hopefully, we learn those lessons sooner rather than later because the sooner we do, the sooner He can move on to the next lesson and the next, and the next . . .

— A LEADERSHIP TIP —

Today, spend a few minutes thinking about the lessons that God is trying to teach you. Focus on one area of your life that needs attention now. And remember, it's always the right time to learn something new.

God is able to take mistakes, when they are committed to Him, and make of them something for our good and for His glory.

Ruth Bell Graham

The wonderful thing about God's schoolroom is that we get to grade our own papers. You see, He doesn't test us so He can learn how well we're doing. He tests us so we can discover how well we're doing.

Charles Swindoll

It's the things you learn after you know it all that really count.

Vance Havner

While chastening is always difficult, if we look to God for the lesson we should learn, we will see spiritual fruit.

Vonette Bright

True learning can take place at every age of life, and it doesn't have to be in the curriculum plan.

Suzanne Dale Ezell

— A LEADER'S PRAYER —
Dear Lord, I have so much to learn. Help me to watch, to listen, to think, and to learn, every day of my life. Amen

So teach us to number our days, that we may gain a heart of wisdom.

Psalm 90:12 NKJV

THE GIFT OF LIFE

Life is a glorious gift from God. Treat it that way.

This day, like every other, is filled to the brim with opportunities, challenges, and choices. But, no choice that you make is more important than the choice you make concerning God. Today, you will either place Him at the center of your life—or not—and the consequences of that choice have implications that are both temporal and eternal.

Sometimes, we don't intentionally neglect God; we simply allow ourselves to become overwhelmed with the demands of everyday life. And then, without our even realizing it, we gradually drift away from the One we need most. Thankfully, God never drifts away from us. He remains always present, always steadfast, always loving.

As you begin this day, place God and His Son where they belong: in your head, in your prayers, on your lips, and in your heart. And then, with God as your guide and companion, let the journey begin.

— A Leadership Tip —

Your life is a priceless opportunity, a gift of incalculable worth. You should thank God for the gift of life . . . and you should use that gift wisely.

Jesus wants Life for us, Life with a capital L.

John Eldredge

You have a glorious future in Christ! Live every moment in His power and love.

Vonette Bright

As I contemplate all the sacrifices required in order to live a life that is totally focused on Jesus Christ and His eternal kingdom, the joy seeps out of my heart onto my face in a smile of deep satisfaction.

Anne Graham Lotz

— A Leader's Prayer —

Lord, as I take the next steps on my life's journey, let me take them with You. You have promised never to leave me or forsake me. You are always with me, protecting me and encouraging me. Whatever this day may bring, I thank You for Your love and for Your strength. Let me lean upon You, Father—and trust You—this day and forever. Amen

The one who is from God listens to God's words. This is why you don't listen, because you are not from God.

John 8:47 HCSB

WISE LEADERS LISTEN TO GOD

Sometimes God speaks loudly and clearly. More often, He speaks in a quiet voice—and if you are wise, you will be listening carefully when He does. To do so, you must carve out quiet moments each day to study His Word and sense His direction.

Can you quiet yourself long enough to listen to your conscience? Are you attuned to the subtle guidance of your intuition? Are you willing to pray sincerely and then to wait quietly for God's response? Hopefully so. Usually God refrains from sending His messages on stone tablets or city billboards. More often, He communicates in subtler ways. If you sincerely desire to hear His voice, you must listen carefully, and you must do so in the silent corners of your quiet, willing heart.

— A LEADERSHIP TIP —

Take time to pray about every major decision. And, remember that prayer is two-way communication with God. Talking to God isn't enough; you should also listen to Him.

When we come to Jesus stripped of pretensions, with a needy spirit, ready to listen, He meets us at the point of need.

Catherine Marshall

We cannot experience the fullness of Christ if we do all the expressing. We must allow God to express His love, will, and truth to us.

Gary Smalley

In prayer, the ear is of first importance. It is of equal importance with the tongue, but the ear must be named first. We must listen to God.

S. D. Gordon

An essential condition of listening to God is that the mind should not be distracted by thoughts of resentment, ill-temper, hatred or vengeance, all of which are comprised in the general term, the wrath of man.

R. V. G. Tasker

— A Leader's Prayer —

Dear Lord, I have so much to learn and You have so much to teach me. Give me the wisdom to be still and the discernment to hear Your voice, today and every day. Amen

When I was a child, I spoke as a child, I understood as a child, I thought as a child; but when I became a man, I put away childish things.

1 Corinthians 13:11 NKJV

GREAT LEADERS CONTINUE TO GROW

The journey toward spiritual maturity lasts a lifetime. As Christian leaders, we can and should continue to grow in the love and the knowledge of our Savior as long as we live. Norman Vincent Peale had the following advice for believers of all ages: "Ask the God who made you to keep remaking you." That advice, of course, is perfectly sound, but often ignored.

When we cease to grow, either emotionally or spiritually, we do ourselves a profound disservice. But, if we study God's Word, if we obey His commandments, and if we live in the center of His will, we will not be "stagnant" believers; we will, instead, be growing Christians . . . and that's exactly what God intends for us to be.

Life is a series of choices. Each day, we make countless decisions that can bring us closer to God . . . or not. When we live according to the principles contained in God's Holy Word, we embark upon a journey of spiritual maturity that results in life abundant and life eternal.

— A LEADERSHIP TIP —

Maturity means that you make wise choices. Immaturity means that you continue making unwise choices . . . it's as simple as that.

We cannot hope to reach Christian maturity in any way other than by yielding ourselves utterly and willingly to His mighty working.

Hannah Whitall Smith

No matter what we are going through, no matter how long the waiting for answers, of one thing we may be sure. God is faithful. He keeps His promises. What He starts, He finishes . . . including His perfect work in us.

Gloria Gaither

Growth in depth and strength and consistency and fruitfulness and ultimately in Christlikeness is only possible when the winds of life are contrary to personal comfort.

Anne Graham Lotz

— A LEADER'S PRAYER —

Dear Lord, let me grow in Your wisdom. When I study Your Word and follow Your commandments, I become a more mature Christian leader. Let me grow up, Lord, and let me keep growing up every day that I live. Amen

Good leaders cultivate honest speech; they love advisors
who tell them the truth.

Proverbs 16:13 MSG

WISE LEADERS FIND
THE RIGHT ROLE MODELS

Here's a simple yet effective way to strengthen your
faith and improve your leadership skills: Choose
role models whose faith in God is strong.

When you emulate godly people, you become
a more godly person yourself. And you become a
more effective leader. That's why you should seek
out mentors who, by their words and their presence,
make you a better person and a better Christian.

Today, as a gift to yourself, select, from your
friends and family members, a mentor whose judgment you trust. Then listen carefully to your mentor's advice and be willing to accept that advice,
even if accepting it requires effort, or pain, or
both. Consider your mentor to be God's gift to you.
Thank God for that gift, and use it for the glory of
His kingdom.

— A LEADERSHIP TIP —

When it comes to mentors, you need them. When
it comes to mentoring, they need you.

God guides through the counsel of good people.

E. Stanley Jones

It takes a wise person to give good advice, but an even wiser person to take it.

Marie T. Freeman

A single word, if spoken in a friendly spirit, may be sufficient to turn one from dangerous error.

Fanny Crosby

No matter how crazy or nutty your life has seemed, God can make something strong and good out of it. He can help you grow wide branches for others to use as shelter.

Barbara Johnson

God often keeps us on the path by guiding us through the counsel of friends and trusted spiritual advisors.

Bill Hybels

— A LEADER'S PRAYER —

Dear Lord, thank You for family members, for friends, and for mentors. When I am troubled, let me turn to them for help, for guidance, for comfort, and for perspective. And Father, let me be a friend and mentor to others, so that my love for You may be reflected in my genuine concern for them. Amen

But Jesus looked at them and said to them, "With men this is impossible, but with God all things are possible."

Matthew 19:26 NKJV

WISE LEADERS KNOW THAT WITH GOD ALL THINGS ARE POSSIBLE

Sometimes, because we are imperfect human beings with limited understanding and limited faith, we place limitations on God. But, God's power has no limitations. God will work miracles in our lives if we trust Him with everything we have and everything we are. When we do, we experience the miraculous results of His endless love and His awesome power.

Miracles, both great and small, are an integral part of everyday life, but usually, we are too busy or too cynical to notice God's handiwork. We don't expect to see miracles, so we simply overlook them.

Do you lack the faith that God can work miracles in your own life? If so, it's time to reconsider. If you have allowed yourself to become a "doubting Thomas," you are attempting to place limitations on a God who has none. Instead of doubting your Heavenly Father, you must trust Him. Then, you must wait and watch . . . because something miraculous is going to happen to you, and it might just happen today.

— A Leadership Tip —

God is in the business of doing miraculous things. You should never be afraid to ask Him for a miracle.

I have been suspected of being what is called a fundamentalist. That is because I never regard any narrative as unhistorical simply on the ground that it includes the miraculous.

C. S. Lewis

When we face an impossible situation, all self-reliance and self-confidence must melt away; we must be totally dependent on Him for the resources.

Anne Graham Lotz

There is Someone who makes possible what seems completely impossible.

Catherine Marshall

Only God can move mountains, but faith and prayer can move God.

E. M. Bounds

— A Leader's Prayer —

Dear Lord, keep me always mindful of Your strength. When I lose hope, give me faith; when others lose hope, let me tell them of Your glory and Your works. Because nothing is impossible for You, I will pray for miracles . . . and I will work for them. Amen

The one who conceals his sins will not prosper, but whoever confesses and renounces them will find mercy.

Proverbs 28:13 HCSB

GREAT LEADERS FACE UP TO THEIR MISTAKES

All leaders make mistakes, and so will you. In fact, Winston Churchill once observed, "Success is going from failure to failure without loss of enthusiasm." What was good for Churchill is also good for you. You should expect to make mistakes—plenty of mistakes—but you should not allow those missteps to rob you of the enthusiasm you need to fulfill God's plan for your life.

We are imperfect people living in an imperfect world; mistakes are simply part of the price we pay for being here. But, even though mistakes are an inevitable part of life's journey, repeated mistakes should not be. When we commit the inevitable blunders of life, we must correct them, learn from them, and pray for the wisdom not to repeat them. When we do, our mistakes become lessons, and our lives become adventures in growth, not stagnation.

Have you made a mistake or three? Of course you have. But here's the big question: have you used your mistakes as stumbling blocks or stepping stones? The answer to that question will determine how well you will perform in the workplace and in every other aspect of your life.

— A Leadership Tip —

When you make a mistake, the time to make things better is now, not later! The sooner you address your problem, the better.

Sin is largely a matter of mistaken priorities. Any sin in us that is cherished, hidden, and not confessed will cut the nerve center of our faith.

Catherine Marshall

God is able to take mistakes, when they are committed to Him, and make of them something for our good and for His glory.

Ruth Bell Graham

Mistakes offer the possibility for redemption and a new start in God's kingdom. No matter what you're guilty of, God can restore your innocence.

Barbara Johnson

— A Leader's Prayer —

Dear Lord, there's a right way to do things and a wrong way to do things. When I do things that are wrong, help me be quick to ask for forgiveness . . . and quick to correct my mistakes. Amen

Then the One seated on the throne said, "Look! I am making everything new."

Revelation 21:5 HCSB

NEW BEGINNINGS

If we sincerely want to change ourselves for the better, we must start on the inside and work our way out from there. Lasting change doesn't occur "out there"; it occurs "in here." It occurs, not in the shifting sands of our own particular circumstances, but in quiet depths of our own hearts.

Life is constantly changing. Our circumstances change; our opportunities change; our responsibilities change; and our relationships change. When we reach the inevitable crossroads of life, we may feel the need to jumpstart our lives . . . or the need to start over from scratch.

Are you in search of a new beginning or, for that matter, a new you? If so, don't expect changing circumstances to miraculously transform you into the person you want to become. Transformation starts with God, and it starts in the silent center of a humble human heart—like yours.

— A Leadership Tip —

If you're graduating into a new phase of life or a new career opportunity, be sure to make God your partner. If you do, He'll guide your steps, He'll help carry your burdens, and He'll help you focus on the things that really matter.

God is not running an antique shop! He is making all things new!

Vance Havner

The amazing thing about Jesus is that He doesn't just patch up our lives, He gives us a brand new sheet, a clean slate to start over, all new.

Gloria Gaither

Like a spring of pure water, God's peace in our hearts brings cleansing and refreshment to our minds and bodies.

Billy Graham

— A Leader's Prayer —

Dear Lord, You have the power to make all things new. Renew my strength, Father, and renew my hope for the future. Today and every day, Lord, let me draw comfort and courage from Your promises and from Your unending love. Amen

Now by this we know that we know Him, if we keep His commandments.

1 John 2:3 NKJV

WISE LEADERS UNDERSTAND THE NEED TO OBEY GOD

Obedience to God is determined, not by words, but by deeds. Talking about righteousness is easy; living righteously is far more difficult, especially in today's temptation-filled world.

Since God created Adam and Eve, we human beings have been rebelling against our Creator. Why? Because we are unwilling to trust God's Word, and we are unwilling to follow His commandments. God has given us a guidebook for righteous living called the Holy Bible. It contains thorough instructions which, if followed, lead to fulfillment, abundance, and salvation. But, if we choose to ignore God's commandments, the results are as predictable as they are tragic.

When we seek righteousness in our own lives—and when we seek the companionship of those who do likewise—we reap the spiritual rewards that God intends for our lives. When we behave ourselves as godly people, we honor God. When we live righteously and according to God's commands, He blesses us in ways that we cannot fully understand.

Do you seek God's peace and His blessings? Then obey Him. When you're faced with a difficult choice or a powerful temptation, seek God's counsel and trust the counsel He gives. Live—and lead—according to His commandments. When you do, you will be blessed today, and tomorrow, and forever.

— A LEADERSHIP TIP —
Because God is just, He rewards good behavior just as surely as He punishes sin. Obedience earns God's pleasure; disobedience doesn't.

Believe and do what God says. The life-changing consequences will be limitless, and the results will be confidence and peace of mind.

Franklin Graham

You may not always see immediate results, but all God wants is your obedience and faithfulness.

Vonette Bright

— A LEADER'S PRAYER —
Dear Lord, today, I will embrace Your love and accept Your wisdom. Guide me, Father, and deliver me from the painful mistakes that I make when I stray from Your commandments. Let me live by Your Word, and let me grow in my faith every day that I live. Amen

Therefore, as we have opportunity, we must work for the good of all, especially for those who belong to the household of faith.

Galatians 6:10 HCSB

TODAY'S OPPORTUNITIES

Are you excited about the opportunities of today and thrilled by the possibilities of tomorrow? Do you confidently expect God to lead you to a place of abundance, peace, and joy? And, when your days on earth are over, do you expect to receive the priceless gift of eternal life? If you trust God's promises, and if you have welcomed God's Son into your heart, then you believe that your future is intensely and eternally bright.

Today, as you prepare to meet the duties of everyday life, pause and consider God's promises. And then think for a moment about the wonderful future that awaits all believers, including you. God has promised that your future is secure. Trust that promise, and celebrate the life of abundance and eternal joy that is now yours through Christ.

— A LEADERSHIP TIP —
When opportunity comes, it's too late to prepare.

John Wooden

Lovely, complicated wrappings / Sheath the gift of one-day-more; / Breathless, I untie the package— / Never lived this day before!

Gloria Gaither

He who waits until circumstances completely favor his undertaking will never accomplish anything.

Martin Luther

God surrounds you with opportunity. You and I are free in Jesus Christ, not to do whatever we want, but to be all that God wants us to be.

Warren Wiersbe

Great opportunities often disguise themselves in small tasks.

Rick Warren

We are all faced with a series of great opportunities, brilliantly disguised as unsolvable problems. Unsolvable without God's wisdom, that is.

Charles Swindoll

— A Leader's Prayer —

Lord, as I take the next steps on my life's journey, let me take them with You. Whatever this day may bring, I thank You for the opportunity to live abundantly. Let me lean upon You, Father—and trust You—this day and forever. Amen

My cup runs over. Surely goodness and mercy shall follow me all the days of my life; and I will dwell in the house of the Lord Forever.

Psalm 23:5-6 NKJV

OPTIMISTIC CHRISTIANITY

Pessimism and Christianity don't mix. Why? Because Christians have every reason to be optimistic about life here on earth and life eternal. As C. H. Spurgeon observed, "Our hope in Christ for the future is the mainstream of our joy." But sometimes, we fall prey to worry, frustration, anxiety, or sheer exhaustion, and our hearts become heavy. What's needed is plenty of rest, a large dose of perspective, and God's healing touch, but not necessarily in that order.

Today, make this promise to yourself and keep it: vow to be a hope-filled Christian. Think optimistically about your life, your profession, and your future. Trust your hopes, not your fears. Take time to celebrate God's glorious creation. And then, when you've filled your heart with hope and gladness, share your optimism with others. They'll be better for it, and so will you. But not necessarily in that order.

— A LEADERSHIP TIP —

Do not build up obstacles in your imagination. Difficulties must be studied and dealt with, but they must not be magnified by fear.

Norman Vincent Peale

It is a remarkable thing that some of the most optimistic and enthusiastic people you will meet are those who have been through intense suffering.

Warren Wiersbe

The Christian lifestyle is not one of legalistic do's and don'ts, but one that is positive, attractive, and joyful.

Vonette Bright

The popular idea of faith is of a certain obstinate optimism: the hope, tenaciously held in the face of trouble, that the universe is fundamentally friendly and things may get better.

J. I. Packer

— A LEADER'S PRAYER —

Lord, let me be an expectant Christian leader. Let me expect the best from You, and let me look for the best in others. If I become discouraged, Father, turn my thoughts and my prayers to You. Let me trust You, Lord, to direct my life. And, let me be Your faithful, hopeful, optimistic servant every day that I live. Amen

He did it with all his heart. So he prospered.

2 Chronicles 31:21 NKJV

WISE LEADERS ARE PASSIONATE ABOUT THEIR LIVES AND THEIR FAITH

The old adage is both familiar and true: We must pray as if everything depended upon God, but work as if everything depended upon us. Yet sometimes, when we are weary and discouraged, we may allow our worries to sap our energy and our hope. God has other intentions. God intends that we pray for things, and He intends that we be willing to work for the things that we pray for. More importantly, God intends that our work should become His work.

Whether you're leading in the workplace, in your church, or just about anyplace else, your success will depend, in large part, upon the passion that you bring to your job. God has created a world in which diligence is rewarded and sloth is not. So whatever you choose to do, do it with commitment, with excitement, with enthusiasm, and with vigor.

God did not create you for a life of mediocrity; He created you for far greater things. Reaching for greater things usually requires work and lots of it, which is perfectly fine with God. After all, He knows that you're up to the task, and He has big plans for you.

— A LEADERSHIP TIP —

When you are passionate about your life, your leadership responsibilities, and your faith . . . great things happen.

One of the great needs in the church today is for every Christian to become enthusiastic about his faith in Jesus Christ.

Billy Graham

Life is too short to spend it being angry, bored, or dull.

Barbara Johnson

Success or failure can be pretty well predicted by the degree to which the heart is fully in it.

John Eldredge

If your heart has grown cold, it is because you have moved away from the fire of His presence.

Beth Moore

— A LEADER'S PRAYER —

Dear Lord, the life that I live and the words that I speak bear testimony to my faith. Make me a faithful and passionate servant of Your Son, and let my testimony be worthy of You. Let my words be sure and true, Lord, and let my actions point others to You. Amen

VERSE 68

One thing I do, forgetting those things which are behind and reaching forward to those things which are ahead, I press toward the goal for the prize of the upward call of God in Christ Jesus.

Philippians 3:13-14 NKJV

WISE LEADERS MAKE PEACE WITH THE PAST

Because you are human, you may be slow to forget yesterday's disappointments. But, if you sincerely seek to focus your hopes and energies on the future, then you must find ways to accept the past, no matter how difficult it may be to do so.

In the third chapter of Philippians, Paul tells us that he chose to focus on the future, not the past. Have you made peace with your past? If so, congratulations. But, if you are mired in the quicksand of regret, it's time to plan your escape. How can you do so? By accepting what has been and by trusting God for what will be.

So, if you're a leader who has not yet made peace with the past, today is the day to declare an end to all hostilities. When you do, you can then turn your thoughts to wondrous promises of God and to the glorious future that He has in store for you.

— A Leadership Tip —

The past is past, so don't invest all your energy there. If you're focused on the past, change your focus. If you're living in the past, it's time to stop living there.

The wise man gives proper appreciation in his life to his past. He learns to sift the sawdust of heritage in order to find the nuggets that make the current moment have any meaning.

Grady Nutt

Yesterday ended last night.

John Maxwell

We set our eyes on the finish line, forgetting the past, and straining toward the mark of spiritual maturity and fruitfulness.

Vonette Bright

— A Leader's Prayer —

Heavenly Father, free me from anger, resentment, and envy. When I am bitter, I cannot feel the peace that You intend for my life. Keep me mindful that forgiveness is Your commandment, and help me accept the past, treasure the present, and trust the future . . . to You. Amen

Do not be deceived: "Bad company corrupts good morals."

1 Corinthians 15:33 HCSB

WISE LEADERS FOLLOW GOD, NOT "THE CROWD"

Rick Warren observed, "Those who follow the crowd usually get lost in it." We know those words to be true, but oftentimes we fail to live by them. Instead of trusting God for guidance, we imitate our friends and suffer the consequences. Instead of seeking to please our Father in heaven, we strive to please our peers, with decidedly mixed results. Instead of doing the right thing, we do the "easy" thing or the "popular" thing. And when we do, we pay a high price for our shortsightedness.

Would you like a time-tested strategy for living—and leading—successfully? Here is a simple formula that is proven and true: don't give in to peer pressure. Period.

Instead of getting lost in the crowd, you should find guidance from God. Does this sound too simple? Perhaps it is simple, but it is also the only way to reap all the marvelous riches that God has in store for you.

— A LEADERSHIP TIP —

A great way to guard your steps is by associating with peers, friends, and coworkers who guard theirs.

For better or worse, you will eventually become more and more like the people you associate with. So why not associate with people who make you better, not worse?

Marie T. Freeman

Comparison is the root of all feelings of inferiority.

James Dobson

Do you want to be wise? Choose wise friends.

Charles Swindoll

Fashion is an enduring testimony to the fact that we live quite consciously before the eyes of others.

John Eldredge

— A LEADER'S PRAYER —

Dear Lord, other people may encourage me to stray from Your path, but I wish to follow in the footsteps of Your Son. Give me the vision to see the right path—and the wisdom to follow it—today and every day of my life. Amen

But God, who is abundant in mercy, because of His great love that He had for us, made us alive with the Messiah even though we were dead in trespasses. By grace you are saved!

Ephesians 2:4-5 HCSB

THE CHAINS OF PERFECTIONISM

Expectations, expectations, expectations! The media delivers an endless stream of messages that tell you how to look, how to behave, and how to dress. The media's expectations are impossible to meet—God's are not. God doesn't expect perfection . . . and neither should you.

If you find yourself bound up by the chains of perfectionism, it's time to ask yourself who you're trying to impress, and why. If you're trying to impress other people, it's time to reconsider your priorities. Your first responsibility is to the Heavenly Father who created you and to His Son who saved you. Then, you bear a powerful responsibility to your family. But, when it comes to meeting society's unrealistic expectations, forget it!

Remember that when you accepted Christ as your Savior, God accepted you for all eternity. Now, it's your turn to accept yourself and your loved ones. When you do, you'll feel a tremendous weight being lifted from your shoulders. After all, pleasing God is simply a matter of obeying His commandments and accepting His Son. But as for pleasing everybody else? That's impossible!

— A Leadership Tip —

There's no such thing as a perfect leader, so if you're caught up in the modern-day push toward perfection, grow up . . . and then lighten up on yourself.

God is so inconceivably good. He's not looking for perfection. He already saw it in Christ. He's looking for affection.

Beth Moore

Excellence is not perfection, but essentially a desire to be strong in the Lord and for the Lord.

Cynthia Heald

A perfectionist resists the truth that growing up in Christ is a process.

Susan Lenzkes

— A Leader's Prayer —

Lord, this world has so many expectations of me, but today I will not seek to meet the world's expectations; I will do my best to meet Your expectations. I will make You my ultimate priority, Lord, by serving You, by praising You, by loving You, and by obeying You. Amen

Do you not know that the runners in a stadium all race, but only one receives the prize? Run in such a way that you may win. Now everyone who competes exercises self-control in everything. However, they do it to receive a perishable crown, but we an imperishable one.

1 Corinthians 9:24-25 HCSB

GREAT LEADERS UNDERSTAND THE POWER OF PERSEVERANCE

In a world filled with roadblocks and stumbling blocks, we need strength, courage, and perseverance. And, as an example of perfect perseverance, we need look no further than our Savior, Jesus.

Jesus finished what He began. Despite the torture He endured, despite the shame of the cross, Jesus was steadfast in His faithfulness to God. We, too, must remain faithful, especially during times of hardship.

Perhaps you are in a hurry for God to reveal His plans for your life. If so, be forewarned: God operates on His own timetable, not yours. Sometimes, God may answer your prayers with silence, and when He does, you must patiently persevere. In times of trouble, you must remain steadfast and trust in the merciful goodness of your Heavenly Father. Whatever your problem, He can handle it. Your job is to keep persevering until He does.

— A Leadership Tip —

To get where you want to go, you must keep on keeping on.

Norman Vincent Peale

Battles are won in the trenches, in the grit and grime of courageous determination; they are won day by day in the arena of life.

Charles Swindoll

Perseverance is more than endurance. It is endurance combined with absolute assurance and certainty that what we are looking for is going to happen.

Oswald Chambers

If things are tough, remember that every flower that ever bloomed had to go through a whole lot of dirt to get there.

Barbara Johnson

— A Leader's Prayer —

Lord, when life is difficult, I am tempted to abandon hope in the future. But You are my God, and I can draw strength from You. When I am exhausted, You energize me. When I am afraid, You give me courage. You are with me, Father, in good times and in bad times. I will persevere in the work that You have placed before me, and I will trust in You forever. Amen

The sensible see danger and take cover; the foolish keep going and are punished.

Proverbs 27:12 HCSB

WISE LEADERS PLAN AHEAD . . . AND WORK HARD

Are you a leader who is willing to plan for the future—and are you willing to work diligently to accomplish the plans that you've made? The Book of Proverbs teaches that the plans of hardworking people (like you) are rewarded.

If you desire to reap a bountiful harvest from life, you must plan for the future while entrusting the final outcome to God. Then, you must do your part to make the future better (by working dutifully), while acknowledging the sovereignty of God's hands over all affairs, including your own.

Are you in a hurry for success to arrive at your doorstep? Don't be. Instead, work carefully, plan thoughtfully, and wait patiently. Remember that you're not the only one working on your behalf: God, too, is at work. And with Him as your partner, your ultimate success is guaranteed.

— A LEADERSHIP TIP —

It isn't that complicated: If you plan your steps carefully, and if you follow your plan conscientiously, you will probably succeed.

Our problem is that we become too easily enamored with our own plans.

Henry Blackaby

We should not be upset when unexpected and upsetting things happen. God, in his wisdom, means to make something of us which we have not yet attained, and He is dealing with us accordingly.

J. I. Packer

Our heavenly Father never takes anything from his children unless he means to give them something better.

George Mueller

When you become consumed by God's call on your life, everything will take on new meaning and significance. You will begin to see every facet of your life—including your pain—as a means through which God can work to bring others to Himself.

Charles Swindoll

God has a plan for your life . . . do you?

Criswell Freeman

— A LEADER'S PRAYER —

Dear Lord, help me accept the past, help me enjoy the present, and help me plan for the future. While I am doing these things, help me to trust You more and more . . . this day and every day. Amen

Rejoice always, pray without ceasing, in everything give thanks; for this is the will of God in Christ Jesus for you.

1 Thessalonians 5:16-18 NKJV

WISE LEADERS PRAY OFTEN

Is prayer an integral part of your daily life, or is it a hit-or-miss habit? Do you "pray without ceasing," or is your prayer life an afterthought? Do you regularly pray in the quiet moments of the early morning, or do you bow your head only when others are watching?

As Christians, we are instructed to pray often. But it is important to note that genuine prayer requires much more than bending our knees and closing our eyes. Heartfelt prayer is an attitude of the heart.

If your prayers have become more a matter of habit than a matter of passion, you're robbing yourself of a deeper relationship with God. How can you rectify this situation? By praying more frequently and more fervently. When you do, God will shower you with His blessings, His grace, and His love.

The quality of your spiritual life will be in direct proportion to the quality of your prayer life: the more you pray, the closer you will feel to God. So today, instead of turning things over in your mind, turn them over to God in prayer. Instead of worrying about your next decision, ask God to lead the way. Don't limit your prayers to the dinner table or the bedside table. Pray constantly about things great and small. God is always listening; it's up to you to do the rest.

— A LEADERSHIP TIP —

There's no corner of your life that's too unimportant to pray about, so pray about everything, including your leadership responsibilities.

It is well said that neglected prayer is the birth-place of all evil.

C. H. Spurgeon

Obedience is the master key to effective prayer.

Billy Graham

Prayer may not get us what we want, but it will teach us to want what we need.

Vance Havner

— A LEADER'S PRAYER —

Dear Lord, make me a person whose constant prayers are pleasing to You. Let me come to You often with concerns both great and small. And, when You answer my prayers, Father, let me trust Your answers, today and forever. Amen

But seek first the kingdom of God and His righteousness, and all these things will be provided for you.

Matthew 6:33 HCSB

WISE LEADERS MAKE GOD THEIR TOP PRIORITY

Jesus made a sacrifice for you. Are you willing to make sacrifices for Him? Can you honestly say that you're passionate about your faith and that you're really following Jesus? Hopefully so. But if you're preoccupied with other things—or if you're strictly a one-day-a-week Christian—then it's time to reorder your priorities.

Nothing is more important than your wholehearted commitment to your Creator and to His only begotten Son. Your faith must never be an afterthought; it must be your ultimate priority, your ultimate possession, and your ultimate passion. You are the recipient of Christ's love. Accept it enthusiastically and share it passionately. Jesus deserves your extreme enthusiasm; the world deserves it; and you deserve the experience of sharing it.

— A LEADERSHIP TIP —

Unless you put first things first, you're bound to finish last. And don't forget that putting first things first means God first and family next.

It's sobering to contemplate how much time, effort, sacrifice, compromise, and attention we give to acquiring and increasing our supply of something that is totally insignificant in eternity.

Anne Graham Lotz

Great relief and satisfaction can come from seeking God's priorities for us in each season, discerning what is "best" in the midst of many noble opportunities, and pouring our most excellent energies into those things.

Beth Moore

Sin is largely a matter of mistaken priorities. Any sin in us that is cherished, hidden, and not confessed will cut the nerve center of our faith.

Catherine Marshall

There were endless demands on Jesus' time. Still he was able to make that amazing claim of "completing the work you gave me to do." (John 17:4 NIV)

Elisabeth Elliot

— A LEADER'S PRAYER —

Lord, let Your priorities be my priorities. Let Your will be my will. Let Your Word be my guide, and let me grow in faith and in wisdom this day and every day. Amen

Your heart must not be troubled. Believe in God; believe also in Me.

John 14:1 HCSB

WISE LEADERS FACE THEIR PROBLEMS AND PRAY ABOUT THEM

Here's a riddle: What is it that is too unimportant to pray about yet too big for God to handle? The answer, of course, is: "nothing." Yet sometimes, when the challenges of the day seem overwhelming, we may spend more time worrying about our troubles than praying about them. And, we may spend more time fretting about our problems than solving them. A far better strategy is to pray as if everything depended entirely upon God and to work as if everything depended entirely upon us.

What we see as problems God sees as opportunities. And if we are to trust Him completely, we must acknowledge that even when our own vision is dreadfully impaired, His vision is perfect. Today and every day, let us trust God by courageously confronting the things that we see as problems and He sees as possibilities.

— A LEADERSHIP TIP —

A problem is an opportunity in work clothes.

Henry J. Kaiser, Jr.

I choose joy. I will refuse the temptation to be cynical; cynicism is the tool of a lazy thinker. I will refuse to see people as anything less than human beings, created by God. I will refuse to see any problem as anything less than an opportunity to see God.

Max Lucado

The happiest people in the world are not those who have no problems, but the people who have learned to live with those things that are less than perfect.

James Dobson

You've got problems; I've got problems; all God's children have got problems. The question is how are you going to deal with them?

John Maxwell

Faith does not eliminate problems. Faith keeps you in a trusting relationship with God in the midst of your problems.

Henry Blackaby

— A LEADER'S PRAYER —

Dear Lord, the things that seem like problems to me may actually be opportunities from You. So today, I will focus not on the challenges I face but on the opportunities I've been given. Amen

You will show me the path of life; in Your presence is fullness of joy; at Your right hand are pleasures forevermore.

Psalm 16:11 NKJV

HE WILL SHOW YOU THE PATH

Life is best lived on purpose. And purpose, like everything else in the universe, begins in the heart of God. Whether you realize it or not, God has a direction for your life, a divine calling, a path along which He intends to lead you. When you welcome God into your heart and establish a genuine relationship with Him, He will begin—and He will continue—to make His purposes known.

Each morning, as the sun rises in the east, you welcome a new day, one that is filled to the brim with opportunities, with possibilities, and with God. As you contemplate God's blessings in your own life, you should prayerfully seek His guidance for the day ahead.

Discovering God's unfolding purpose for your life is a daily journey, a journey guided by the teachings of God's Holy Word. As you reflect upon God's promises and upon the meaning that those promises hold for you, ask God to lead you throughout the coming day. Let your Heavenly Father direct your steps; concentrate on what God wants you to do now, and leave the distant future in hands that are far more capable than your own: His hands.

Sometimes, God's intentions will be clear to you; other times, God's plan will seem uncertain at best. But even on those difficult days when you are unsure which way to turn, you must never lose sight of these overriding facts: God created you for a reason; He has important work for you to do; and He's waiting patiently for you to do it.

— A LEADERSHIP TIP —

God has a plan for your life, a definite purpose that you can fulfill . . . or not. Your challenge is to pray for God's guidance and to follow wherever He leads.

When God speaks to you through the Bible, prayer, circumstances, the church, or in some other way, he has a purpose in mind for your life.

Henry Blackaby and Claude King

— A LEADER'S PRAYER —

Dear Lord, I know that You have a purpose for my life, and I will seek that purpose today and every day that I live. Let my actions be pleasing to You, and let me share Your Good News with a world that so desperately needs Your healing hand and the salvation of Your Son. Amen

Be still, and know that I am God....

Psalm 46:10 KJV

BE STILL

We live in a noisy world, a world filled with distractions, frustrations, obligations, and complications. But we must not allow our clamorous world to separate us from God's peace. Instead, we must "be still" so that we might sense the presence of God.

If we are to maintain righteous minds and compassionate hearts, we must take time each day for prayer and for meditation. We must make ourselves still in the presence of our Creator. We must quiet our minds and our hearts so that we might sense God's love, God's will, and God's Son.

Has the busy pace of life robbed you of the peace that might otherwise be yours through Jesus Christ? If so, it's time to reorder your priorities. Nothing is more important than the time you spend with your Savior. So be still and claim the inner peace that is your spiritual birthright: the peace of Jesus Christ. It is offered freely; it has been paid for in full; it is yours for the asking. So ask. And then share.

— A LEADERSHIP TIP —

Be still and listen to God. He has something important to say to you.

Since the quiet hour spent with God is the preacher's power-house, the devil centers his attention on that source of strength.

Vance Havner

Quiet time is giving God your undivided attention for a predetermined amount of time for the purpose of talking to and hearing from Him.

Charles Stanley

Let this be your chief object in prayer, to realize the presence of your heavenly Father. Let your watchword be: Alone with God.

Andrew Murray

When we are in the presence of God, removed from distractions, we are able to hear him more clearly, and a secure environment has been established for the young and broken places in our hearts to surface.

John Eldredge

— A Leader's Prayer —

Lord, Your Holy Word is a light unto the world; let me study it, trust it, and share it with all who cross my path. Let me discover You, Father, in the quiet moments of the day. And, in all that I say and do, help me to be a worthy witness as I share the Good News of Your perfect Son and Your perfect Word. Amen

VERSE 78

Therefore if anyone is in Christ, he is a new creature; the old things passed away; behold, new things have come.

2 Corinthians 5:17 HCSB

WISE LEADERS KNOW THAT GOD OFFERS RENEWAL

When we genuinely lift our hearts and prayers to God, He renews our strength. Are you almost too weary to lift your head? Then bow it. Offer your concerns and your fears to your Father in Heaven. He is always at your side, offering His love and His strength.

Are you troubled or anxious? Take your anxieties to God in prayer. Are you weak or worried? Delve deeply into God's Holy Word and sense His presence in the quiet moments of the early morning. Are you spiritually exhausted? Call upon fellow believers to support you, and call upon Christ to renew your spirit and your life. Your Savior will never let you down. To the contrary, He will always lift you up if you ask Him to. So what, dear friend, are you waiting for?

— A LEADERSHIP TIP —

God can make all things new, including you. When you are weak or worried, God can renew your spirit. Your task is to let Him.

Walking with God leads to receiving his intimate counsel, and counseling leads to deep restoration.

John Eldredge

For centuries now, Christians have poured out their hearts to the Lord and found treasured moments of refuge.

Bill Hybels

Troubles we bear trustfully can bring us a fresh vision of God and a new outlook on life, an outlook of peace and hope.

Billy Graham

— A LEADER'S PRAYER —

Dear Lord, sometimes I grow weary; sometimes I am discouraged; sometimes I am fearful. Yet when I turn my heart and my prayers to You, I am secure. Renew my strength, Father, and let me draw comfort and courage from Your promises and from Your unending love. Amen

VERSE 79

If we confess our sins, He is faithful and righteous to forgive us our sins and to cleanse us from all unrighteousness.

1 John 1:9 HCSB

REAL REPENTANCE

Who among us has sinned? All of us. But, God calls upon us to turn away from sin by following His commandments. And the good news is this: When we do ask God's forgiveness and turn our hearts to Him, He forgives us absolutely and completely.

Genuine repentance requires more than simply offering God apologies for our misdeeds. Real repentance may start with feelings of sorrow and remorse, but it ends only when we turn away from the sin that has heretofore distanced us from our Creator. In truth, we offer our most meaningful apologies to God, not with our words, but with our actions. As long as we are still engaged in sin, we may be "repenting," but we have not fully "repented."

Is there an aspect of your life that is distancing you from your God? If so, ask for His forgiveness, and—just as importantly—stop sinning. Then, wrap yourself in the protection of God's Word. When you do, you will be secure.

— A LEADERSHIP TIP —

If you're engaged in behavior that is displeasing to God, today is the day to stop. First, confess your sins to God. Then, ask Him what actions you should take in order to make things right again.

Repentance is among other things a sincere apology to God for distrusting Him so long, and faith is throwing oneself upon Christ in complete confidence.

A. W. Tozer

Four marks of true repentance are: acknowledgement of wrong, willingness to confess it, willingness to abandon it, and willingness to make restitution.

Corrie ten Boom

— A LEADER'S PRAYER —

When I stray from Your commandments, Lord, I must not only confess my sins, I must also turn from them. When I fall short, help me to change. When I reject Your Word and Your will for my life, guide me back to Your side. Forgive my sins, Dear Lord, and help me live according to Your plan for my life. Your plan is perfect, Father; I am not. Let me trust in You. Amen

Come to me, all you who are weary and burdened, and I will give you rest. Take my yoke upon you and learn from me, for I am gentle and humble in heart, and you will find rest for your souls. For my yoke is easy and my burden is light.

Matthew 11:28-30 NIV

ENOUGH REST?

Even the most inspired Christian leaders can, from time to time, find themselves running on empty. The demands of daily life can drain us of our strength and rob us of the joy that is rightfully ours in Christ. When we find ourselves tired, discouraged, or worse, there is a source from which we can draw the power needed to recharge our spiritual batteries. That source is God.

God intends that His children lead joyous lives filled with abundance and peace. But sometimes, abundance and peace seem very far away. It is then that we must turn to God for renewal, and when we do, He will restore us.

God expects us to work hard, but He also intends for us to rest. When we fail to take the rest that we need, we do a disservice to ourselves and to our families.

Is your spiritual battery running low? Is your energy on the wane? Are your emotions frayed? If so, it's time to turn your thoughts and your prayers to God. And when you're finished, it's time to rest.

— A LEADERSHIP TIP —

It takes energy to be a good leader; exhaustion is not God's way. A well-rested Christian leader can be a much more effective worker for God.

Jesus gives us the ultimate rest, the confidence we need, to escape the frustration and chaos of the world around us.

Billy Graham

Satan does some of his worst work on exhausted Christians when nerves are frayed and their minds are faint.

Vance Havner

Jesus taught us by example to get out of the rat race and recharge our batteries.

Barbara Johnson

— A LEADER'S PRAYER —

Dear Lord, when I'm tired, give me the wisdom to do the smart thing: give me the wisdom to put my head on my pillow and rest! Amen

Six days shall work be done, but the seventh day is a Sabbath of solemn rest, a holy convocation. You shall do no work on it; it is the Sabbath of the Lord in all your dwellings.

Leviticus 23:3 NKJV

WISE LEADERS KEEP THE SABBATH

When God gave Moses the Ten Commandments, it became perfectly clear that our Heavenly Father intends for us to make the Sabbath a holy day, a day for worship, for contemplation, for fellowship, and for rest. Yet we live in a seven-day-a-week world, a world that all too often treats Sunday as a regular workday.

One way to demonstrate Christian leadership is by giving God at least one day each week. If you carve out the time for a day of worship and praise, you'll be amazed at the impact it will have on the rest of your week. But if you fail to honor God's day, if you treat the Sabbath as a day to work or a day to party, you'll miss out on a harvest of blessings that is only available one day each week.

How does your family observe the Lord's day? When church is over, do you treat Sunday like any other day of the week? If so, it's time to think long and hard about your family's schedule and your family's priorities. And if you've been treating Sunday as just another day, it's time to break that habit. When Sunday rolls around, don't try to fill every spare moment. Take time to rest . . . Father's orders!

— A Leadership Tip —

Today, think about new ways that you can honor God on the Sabbath. The Sabbath is unlike the other six days of the week, and it's up to you to treat it that way.

Jesus gives us the ultimate rest, the confidence we need, to escape the frustration and chaos of the world around us.

Billy Graham

One reason so much American Christianity is a mile wide and an inch deep is that Christians are simply tired. Sometimes you need to kick back and rest for Jesus' sake.

Dennis Swanberg

— A Leader's Prayer —

Dear Lord, I thank You for the Sabbath day, a day when I can worship You and praise Your Son. I will keep the Sabbath as a holy day, a day when I can honor You. Amen

Honor His holy name; let the hearts of those who seek the Lord rejoice. Search for the Lord and for His strength; seek His face always.

1 Chronicles 16:10-11 HCSB

WISE LEADERS CONTINUALLY SEEK GOD

Sometimes, in the crush of our daily duties, God may seem far away, but He is not. God is everywhere we have ever been and everywhere we will ever go. He is with us night and day; He knows our thoughts and our prayers. And, when we earnestly seek Him, we will find Him because He is here, waiting patiently for us to reach out to Him.

If you have been touched by the transforming love of Jesus, then you have every reason to live courageously. After all, Christ has already won the ultimate battle—and He won it for you—on the cross at Calvary. Still, even if you are a dedicated Christian, you may find yourself discouraged by the inevitable disappointments and tragedies that occur in the lives of believers and non-believers alike.

The next time you find your courage tested to the limit, lean upon God's promises. Trust His Son. Remember that God is always near and that He is your protector and your deliverer. And please remember that no matter your circumstances, and no matter your leadership responsibilities, God will never leave you. He is always present, always loving, always ready to comfort and protect.

— A Leadership Tip —

God is searching for you; it's up to you—and you alone—to open your heart to Him.

Thirsty hearts are those whose longings have been wakened by the touch of God within them.

A. W. Tozer

Some people pray just to pray, and some people pray to know God.

Andrew Murray

But I'm convinced the best way to cope with change, ironically enough, is to get to know a God who doesn't change, One who provides an anchor in the swirling seas of change.

Bill Hybels

— A Leader's Prayer —

Dear Lord, in the quiet moments of this day, I will turn my thoughts and prayers to You. In these silent moments, I will seek Your presence and Your will for my life, knowing that when I accept Your peace, I will be blessed today and throughout eternity. Amen

*For You have made him a little lower than the angels,
and You have crowned him with glory and honor.*

Psalm 8:5 NKJV

WISE LEADERS UNDERSTAND THE IMPORTANCE OF BUILDING A HEALTHY SELF-IMAGE

Sometimes, it's hard to feel good about yourself, especially when you live in a society that keeps sending out the message that you've got to be perfect.

Are you your own worst critic? And in response to that criticism, are you constantly trying to transform yourself into a person who meets society's expectations, but not God's expectations? If so, it's time to become a little more understanding of the person you see whenever you look into the mirror.

Millions of words have been written about various ways to improve self-esteem. Yet, maintaining a healthy self-image is, to a surprising extent, a matter of doing three things: 1. Obeying God, 2. Thinking healthy thoughts, and 3. Becoming passionate about doing things that please your Creator and yourself. When you take these three steps, your self-image will tend to take care of itself—and your life will serve as an enduring testimony to the changes that God makes in the lives of faithful followers like you.

— A Leadership Tip —

Don't make the mistake of selling yourself short. No matter the size of your challenges, you can be sure that you and God, working together, can handle them.

You are valuable just because you exist. Not because of what you do or what you have done, but simply because you are.

Max Lucado

If you ever put a price tag on yourself, it would have to read "Jesus" because that is what God paid to save you.

Josh McDowell

Your self-image need not be permanently damaged by the circumstances of life. It can be recast when there is an infusion of new life in Jesus Christ.

Ed Young

Give yourself a gift today: be present with yourself. God is. Enjoy your own personality. God does.

Barbara Johnson

— A Leader's Prayer —

Dear Lord, keep me mindful that I am a special person, created by You, loved by You, and saved by Your Son. Amen

We must do the works of Him who sent Me while it is day. Night is coming when no one can work.

John 9:4 HCSB

WISE LEADERS SERVE GOD

We live in a world that glorifies power, prestige, fame, and money. But the words of Jesus teach us that the most esteemed men and women in this world are not the self-congratulatory masters of society but are, instead, the humblest of servants.

Are you willing to become a humble servant-leader for Christ? Are you willing to pitch in and make the world a better place, or are you determined to keep all your blessings to yourself. The answers to these questions will determine the quality of your leadership and the direction of your life.

Today, you may feel the temptation to take more than you give. You may be tempted to withhold your generosity. Or you may be tempted to build yourself up in the eyes of your associates. Resist those temptations. Instead, serve others quietly and without fanfare. Find a need and fill it . . . humbly. Lend a helping hand . . . anonymously. Share a word of kindness . . . with quiet sincerity. As you go about your daily activities, remember that the Savior of all humanity made Himself a servant, and we, as His followers, must do no less.

— A LEADERSHIP TIP —

Christian leaders are servant-leaders. The direction of your steps and the quality of your life will be determined by the level of your service.

No life can surpass that of a man who quietly continues to serve God in the place where providence has placed him.

C. H. Spurgeon

A Christian is a perfectly free lord of all, subject to none. A Christian is a perfectly dutiful servant of all, subject to all.

Martin Luther

If doing a good act in public will excite others to do more good, then "Let your Light shine to all." Miss no opportunity to do good.

John Wesley

— A LEADER'S PRAYER —

Father in heaven, when Jesus humbled Himself and became a servant, He also became an example for His followers. Today, as I serve my family, my friends, and my coworkers, I do so in the name of Jesus. Guide my steps, Father, and let my service be pleasing to You. Amen

Now godliness with contentment is great gain. For we brought nothing into this world, and it is certain we can carry nothing out. And having food and clothing, with these we shall be content.

1 Timothy 6:6-8 NKJV

WISE LEADERS KEEP IT SIMPLE

You live in a world where simplicity is in short supply. Think for a moment about the complexity of your everyday life and compare it to the lives of your ancestors. Certainly, you are the beneficiary of many technological innovations, but those innovations have a price: in all likelihood, your world is highly complex. Consider the following:

1. From the moment you wake up in the morning until the time you lay your head on the pillow at night, you are the target of an endless stream of advertising information. Each message is intended to grab your attention in order to convince you to purchase things you didn't know you needed (and probably don't!).

2. Essential aspects of your life and career are subject to an ever-increasing flood of rules and regulations.

3. Unless you take firm control of your time, your life, and your organization, you may be overwhelmed by an ever-increasing tidal wave of complexity that threatens your success.

Your Heavenly Father understands the joy of living simply, and so should you. So do yourself, your family, and your associates a favor: keep things as simple as possible. Simplicity is, indeed, genius. By simplifying things, you are destined to improve them.

— A LEADERSHIP TIP —

Simplicity and peace are two concepts that are closely related. Complexity and peace are not.

Prescription for a happier and healthier life: resolve to slow down your pace; learn to say no gracefully; resist the temptation to chase after more pleasure, more hobbies, and more social entanglements.

James Dobson

Efficiency is enhanced not by what we accomplish but more often by what we relinquish.

Charles Swindoll

— A LEADER'S PRAYER —

Dear Lord, help me understand the joys of simplicity. Life is complicated enough without my adding to the confusion. Wherever I happen to be, help me to keep it simple—very simple. Amen

A word fitly spoken is like apples of gold in settings of silver.

Proverbs 25:11 NKJV

WISE LEADERS MEASURE THEIR WORDS CAREFULLY

Throughout the Book of Proverbs, we are reminded that the words we speak have great power. If our words are encouraging, we can lift others up; if our words are hurtful, we can hold others back. So, if we hope to solve more problems than we start, we must measure our words carefully.

Sometimes, even the most thoughtful among us speak first and think second (with decidedly mixed results). A far better strategy, of course, is to do the more difficult thing: to think first and to speak next.

Do you want to be a leader who serves as a constant source of encouragement to others? And, do you seek to be a worthy ambassador for Christ? If so, you must speak words that are worthy of your Savior. So avoid angry outbursts and impulsive outpourings. Instead, speak words of encouragement and hope to a world that desperately needs both.

— A LEADERSHIP TIP —

Wise leaders pay careful attention to the words they speak. So, measure your words carefully and prayerfully.

The great test of a man's character is his tongue.

Oswald Chambers

Change the heart, and you change the speech.

Warren Wiersbe

Part of good communication is listening with the eyes well as with the ears.

Josh McDowell

The best use of life is love. The best expression of love is time. The best time to love is now.

Rick Warren

A little kindly advice is better than a great deal of scolding.

Fanny Crosby

— A Leader's Prayer —

Dear Lord, You have commanded me to choose my words carefully so that I might be a source of encouragement and hope to all whom I meet. Keep me mindful, Lord, that I have influence on many people. Let the words that I speak today be worthy of the One who has saved me forever. Amen

Depend on the Lord and his strength; always go to him for help. Remember the miracles he has done; remember his wonders and his decisions.

Psalm 105:4-5 NCV

STRENGTH FROM GOD

Today, like every other day, is literally brimming with possibilities. Whether we realize it or not, God is always working in us and through us; our job is to let Him do His work without undue interference. Yet we are imperfect beings who, because of our limited vision, often resist God's will. And oftentimes, because of our stubborn insistence on squeezing too many activities into a 24-hour day, we allow ourselves to become exhausted, or frustrated, or both.

Are you tired or troubled? Turn your heart toward God in prayer. Are you weak or worried? Take the time—or, more accurately, make the time—to delve deeply into God's Holy Word. Are you spiritually depleted? Call upon fellow believers to support you, and call upon Christ to renew your spirit and your life. Are you simply overwhelmed by the demands of the day? Pray for the wisdom to simplify your life.

When you do these things, you'll discover that the Creator of the universe stands always ready and always able to create a new sense of wonderment and joy in you.

— A LEADERSHIP TIP —

When you are tired, fearful, or discouraged, God can restore your strength.

The same God who empowered Samson, Gideon, and Paul seeks to empower my life and your life, because God hasn't changed.

Bill Hybels

We have a God who delights in impossibilities.

Andrew Murray

A divine strength is given to those who yield themselves to the Father and obey what He tells them to do.

Warren Wiersbe

— A LEADER'S PRAYER —

Dear Lord, I will turn to You for strength. When my leadership responsibilities seem overwhelming, I will trust You to give me courage and perspective. Today and every day, I will look to You as the ultimate source of my hope, my strength, my peace, and my salvation. Amen

Commit your activities to the Lord and your plans will be achieved.

Proverbs 16:3 HCSB

DEFINING SUCCESS

How do you define success? Do you define it as the accumulation of material possessions or the adulation of your neighbors? If so, you need to reorder your priorities. Genuine success has little to do with fame or fortune; it has everything to do with God's gift of love and His promise of salvation.

If you have accepted Christ as your personal Savior, you are already a towering success in the eyes of God, but there is still more that you can do. Your task—as a believer who has been touched by the Creator's grace—is to accept the spiritual abundance and peace that He offers through the person of His Son. Then, you can share the healing message of God's love and His abundance with a world that desperately needs both. When you do, you have reached the pinnacle of success.

— A LEADERSHIP TIP —

Don't let the world define success for you. Only God can do that.

We, as believers, must allow God to define success. And, when we do, God blesses us with His love and His grace.

Jim Gallery

Success or failure can be pretty well predicted by the degree to which the heart is fully in it.

John Eldredge

Often, attitude is the only difference between success and failure.

John Maxwell

There's not much you can't achieve or endure if you know God is walking by your side. Just remember: Someone knows, and Someone cares.

Bill Hybels

Success and happiness are not destinations. They are exciting, never-ending journeys.

Zig Ziglar

— A Leader's Prayer —

Dear Lord, let Your priorities be my priorities. Let Your will be my will. Let Your Word be my guide, and keep me mindful that genuine success is a result, not of the world's approval, but of Your approval. Amen

We have different gifts, according to the grace given us. If it is leadership, let him govern diligently; if it is showing mercy, let him do it cheerfully.

Romans 12:6, 8 NIV

USING YOUR TALENTS

The old saying is both familiar and true: "What we are is God's gift to us; what we become is our gift to God." Each of us possesses special talents, gifted by God, that can be nurtured carefully or ignored totally. Our challenge, of course, is to use our abilities to the greatest extent possible and to use them in ways that honor our Savior.

Are you using your natural talents to make God's world a better place? If so, congratulations. But if you have gifts that you have not fully explored and developed, perhaps you need to have a chat with the One who gave you those gifts in the first place. Your talents are priceless treasures offered from your Heavenly Father. Use them. After all, an obvious way to say "thank you" to the Giver is to use the gifts He has given.

— A LEADERSHIP TIP —
God has given you a unique array of talents and opportunities. The rest is up to you.

You are a unique blend of talents, skills, and gifts, which makes you an indispensable member of the body of Christ.

Charles Stanley

In the great orchestra we call life, you have an instrument and a song, and you owe it to God to play them both sublimely.

Max Lucado

You are the only person on earth who can use your ability.

Zig Ziglar

One thing taught large in the Holy Scriptures is that while God gives His gifts freely, He will require a strict accounting of them at the end of the road. Each man is personally responsible for his store, be it large or small, and will be required to explain his use of it before the judgment seat of Christ.

A. W. Tozer

— A LEADER'S PRAYER —

Lord, You have given all of us talents, and I am no exception. You have blessed me with a gift—let me discover it, nurture it, and use it for the glory of Your Kingdom. I will share my gifts with the world, and I will give praise to You, the Giver of all things good. Amen

No temptation has overtaken you except such as is common to man; but God is faithful, who will not allow you to be tempted beyond what you are able, but with the temptation will also make the way of escape, that you may be able to bear it.

1 Corinthians 10:13 NKJV

RESISTING TEMPTATION

It's inevitable: today you will be tempted by somebody or something—in fact, you will probably be tempted many times. Why? Because you live in a world that is filled to the brim with temptations! Some of these temptations are small; eating a second scoop of ice cream, for example, is enticing but not very dangerous. Other temptations, however, are not nearly so harmless.

The devil is working 24/7, and he's causing pain and heartache in more ways than ever before. We, as believers, must remain watchful and strong. And the good news is this: When it comes to fighting Satan, we are never alone. God is always with us, and He gives us the power to resist temptation whenever we ask Him to give us strength.

In a letter to believers, Peter offered a warning: "Your adversary, the devil, prowls around like a roaring lion, seeking someone to devour" (1 Peter 5:8 NASB). As Christians, we must take that warning seriously, and we must behave accordingly.

— A LEADERSHIP TIP —

Because you live in a temptation-filled world, you must guard your eyes, your thoughts, and your heart—all day, every day.

It is easier to stay out of temptation than to get out of it.

Rick Warren

In the worst temptations nothing can help us but faith that God's Son has put on flesh, sits at the right hand of the Father, and prays for us. There is no mightier comfort.

Martin Luther

Most Christians do not know or fully realize that the adversary of our lives is Satan and that his main tool is our flesh, our old nature.

Bill Bright

— A LEADER'S PRAYER —

Dear Lord, this world is filled with temptations, distractions, and frustrations. When I turn my thoughts away from You and Your Word, Lord, I suffer bitter consequences. But, when I trust in Your commandments, I am safe. Direct my path far from the temptations and distractions of the world. Let me discover Your will and follow it, Dear Lord, this day and always. Amen

Thanks be to God for His indescribable gift.

2 Corinthians 9:15 HCSB

A THANKFUL HEART

Sometimes, life here on earth can be complicated, demanding, and frustrating. When the demands of life and leadership leave us rushing from place to place with scarcely a moment to spare, we may fail to pause and thank our Creator for the countless blessings He bestows upon us. But, whenever we neglect to give proper thanks to the Giver of all things good, we suffer because of our misplaced priorities.

As believers who have been saved by a risen Christ, we are blessed beyond human comprehension. We who have been given so much should make thanksgiving a habit, a regular part of our daily routines. Of course, God's gifts are too numerous to count, but we should attempt to count them nonetheless. We owe our Heavenly Father everything, including our eternal praise . . . starting right now.

— A LEADERSHIP TIP —

By speaking words of thanksgiving and praise, you honor the Father and you protect your heart against the twin evils of apathy and ingratitude.

The words "thank" and "think" come from the same root word. If we would think more, we would thank more.

Warren Wiersbe

God often keeps us on the path by guiding us through the counsel of friends and trusted spiritual advisors.

Bill Hybels

Though I know intellectually how vulnerable I am to pride and power, I am the last one to know when I succumb to their seduction. That's why spiritual Lone Rangers are so dangerous—and why we must depend on trusted brothers and sisters who love us enough to tell us the truth.

Chuck Colson

Thanksgiving is good but Thanksliving is better.

Jim Gallery

— A Leader's Prayer —

Lord, let me be a thankful Christian. Your blessings are priceless and eternal. I praise You, Lord, for Your gifts and, most of all, for Your Son. Your love endures forever. I will offer You my heartfelt thanksgiving this day and throughout all eternity. Amen

Finally, brethren, whatever things are true, whatever things are noble, whatever things are just, whatever things are pure, whatever things are lovely, whatever things are of good report, if there is any virtue and if there is anything praiseworthy—meditate on these things.

Philippians 4:8 NKJV

THE DIRECTION OF YOUR THOUGHTS

How will you direct your thoughts today? Will you obey the words of Philippians 4:8 by dwelling upon those things that are true, noble, and just? Or will you allow your thoughts to be hijacked by the negativity that seems to dominate our troubled world?

Are you fearful, angry, bored, or worried? Are you so preoccupied with the concerns of this day that you fail to thank God for the promise of eternity? Are you confused, bitter, or pessimistic? If so, God wants to have a little talk with you.

God intends that you be an ambassador for Him, an enthusiastic, hope-filled Christian leader. But God won't force you to adopt a positive attitude. It's up to you to think positively about your blessings and opportunities . . . or not. So, today and every day hereafter, celebrate this life that God has given you by focusing your thoughts and your energies upon "things that are excellent and worthy of praise." Today, count your blessings instead of your hardships. And thank the Giver of all things good for gifts that are simply too numerous to count.

— A Leadership Tip —

Either you can control your thoughts, or they most certainly will control you.

It is the thoughts and intents of the heart that shape a person's life.

John Eldredge

Whether we think of, or speak to, God, whether we act or suffer for him, all is prayer when we have no other object than his love and the desire of pleasing him.

John Wesley

— A Leader's Prayer —

Dear Lord, I will focus on Your love, Your power, Your promises, and Your Son. When I am weak, I will turn to You for strength; when I am worried, I will turn to You for comfort; when I am troubled, I will turn to You for patience and perspective. Help me guard my thoughts, Lord, so that I may honor You this day and forever. Amen

VERSE 93

This is the day which the LORD hath made; we will rejoice and be glad in it.

Psalm 118:24 KJV

WISE LEADERS CELEBRATE THE GIFT OF LIFE

Today is a non-renewable resource—once it's gone, it's gone forever. Our responsibility, as thoughtful believers, is to use this day in the service of God's will and in the service of His people. When we do so, we enrich our own lives and the lives of those whom we love.

God has richly blessed us, and He wants you to rejoice in His gifts. That's why this day—and each day that follows—should be a time of prayer and celebration as we consider the Good News of God's free gift: salvation through Jesus Christ.

What do you expect from the day ahead? Are you expecting God to do wonderful things, or are you living beneath a cloud of apprehension and doubt? The familiar words of Psalm 118:24 remind us that every day is a cause for celebration. Our duty, as believers, is to rejoice in God's marvelous creation.

Today, celebrate the life that God has given you. Today, put a smile on your face, kind words on your lips, and a song in your heart. Be generous with your praise and free with your encouragement. And then, when you have celebrated life to the fullest, invite your friends to do likewise. After all, this is God's day, and He has given us clear instructions for its use. We are commanded to rejoice and be glad. So, with no further ado, let the celebration begin.

— A Leadership Tip —
Today is a wonderful, one-of-a-kind gift from God. Treat it that way.

When we truly walk with God throughout our day, life slowly starts to fall into place.

Bill Hybels

Christ is the secret, the source, the substance, the center, and the circumference of all true and lasting gladness.

Mrs. Charles E. Cowman

— A Leader's Prayer —
Dear Lord, You have given me another day of life; let me celebrate this day, and let me use it according to Your plan. I come to You today with faith in my heart and praise on my lips. I praise You, Father, for the gift of life and for the family, friends, and coworkers who make my life rich. Enable me to live each moment to the fullest, totally involved in Your will. Amen

Trust in the Lord with all your heart, and lean not on your own understanding.

Proverbs 3:5 NKJV

WISE LEADERS TRUST GOD

It's easy to talk about trusting God, but when it comes to actually trusting Him, that's considerably harder. Genuine trust in God requires more than words; it requires a willingness to follow God's lead and a willingness to obey His commandments. (These, by the way, are not easy things to do.)

Have you spent more time talking about Christ than walking in His footsteps? If so, God wants to have a little chat with you. And, if you're unwilling to talk to Him, He may take other actions in order to grab your attention.

Thankfully, whenever you're willing to talk with God, He's willing to listen. And, the instant that you decide to place Him squarely in the center of your life, He will respond to that decision with blessings that are too unexpected to predict and too numerous to count.

The next time you find your courage tested to the limit, lean upon God's promises. Trust His Son. Remember that God is always near and that He is your protector and your deliverer. When you are worried, anxious, or afraid, call upon Him. God can handle your troubles infinitely better than you can, so turn them over to Him. Remember that God rules both mountaintops and valleys—with limitless wisdom and love—now and forever.

— A LEADERSHIP TIP —

Because God is trustworthy—and because He has made promises to you that He intends to keep—you are protected.

God is God. He knows what he is doing. When you can't trace his hand, trust his heart.

Max Lucado

The hope we have in Jesus is the anchor for the soul—something sure and steadfast, preventing drifting or giving way, lowered to the depth of God's love.

Franklin Graham

— A LEADER'S PRAYER —

Dear Lord, let my faith be in You, and in You alone. Without You, I am weak, but when I trust You, I am protected. In every aspect of my life, Father, let me place my hope and my trust in Your infinite wisdom and Your boundless grace. Amen

And you shall know the truth, and the truth shall make you free.

John 8:32 NKJV

TRUTH WITH A CAPITAL T

God is vitally concerned with truth. His Word teaches the truth; His Spirit reveals the truth; His Son leads us to the truth. When we open our hearts to God, and when we allow His Son to rule over our thoughts and our lives, God reveals Himself, and we come to understand the truth about ourselves and the Truth (with a capital T) about God's gift of grace.

The familiar words of John 8:32 remind us that when we come to know God's Truth, we are liberated. Have you been liberated by that Truth? And are you living—and leading—in accordance with the eternal truths that you find in God's Holy Word? Hopefully so.

Today, as you fulfill the responsibilities that God has placed before you, ask yourself this question: "Do my thoughts and actions bear witness to the ultimate Truth that God has placed in my heart, or am I allowing the pressures of everyday life to overwhelm me?" It's a profound question that deserves an answer . . . now.

— A Leadership Tip —

Jesus offers you the Truth with a Capital T. How you respond to His Truth will determine the direction—and the destination—of your life.

We have in Jesus Christ a perfect example of how to put God's truth into practice.

Bill Bright

For Christians, God himself is the only absolute; truth and ethics are rooted in his character.

Charles Colson

Truth will triumph. The Father of truth will win, and the followers of truth will be saved.

Max Lucado

God will see to it that we understand as much truth as we are willing to obey.

Elisabeth Elliot

— A Leader's Prayer —

Heavenly Father, let me trust in Your Word and in Your Son. Jesus said He was the truth, and I believe Him. Make Jesus the standard for truth in my life so that I might be a worthy example to others and a worthy servant to You. Amen

*Sow righteousness for yourselves and reap faithful love;
break up your untilled ground. It is time to seek the Lord
until He comes and sends righteousness on you like the
rain.*

Hosea 10:12 HCSB

THE VALUE SYSTEM
YOU CAN DEPEND ON

From the time your alarm clock wakes you in the
morning until the moment you lay your head on
the pillow at night, your actions are guided by the
values that you hold most dear. And if you intend
to experience God's blessings, you'll make sure that
your values are shaped by His promises.

Society seeks to impose its own set of values
upon you, your family, and your associates, but often, these values are contrary to God's Word (and
thus contrary to your own best interests). The
world promises happiness, contentment, prosper-
ity, and abundance. But genuine abundance is not
a by-product of worldly possessions or status; it is a
by-product of your thoughts, your actions, and your
relationship with the Creator.

The world's promises are incomplete and de-
ceptive; God's promises are unfailing. Your challenge, then, is to build your value system upon the
value system that never fails: God's value system.

— A LEADERSHIP TIP —

You can have the values that the world holds dear, or you can have the values that God holds dear, but you can't have both. The decision is yours . . . and so are the consequences.

Blessed are those who know what on earth they are here on earth to do and set themselves about the business of doing it.

Max Lucado

Sadly, family problems and even financial problems are seldom the real problem, but often the symptom of a weak or nonexistent value system.

Dave Ramsey

You will get untold flak for prioritizing God's revealed and present will for your life over man's . . . but, boy, is it worth it.

Beth Moore

Discrepancies between values and practices create chaos in a person's life.

John Maxwell

— A LEADER'S PRAYER —

Lord, help me value the things in this world that are really valuable: my life, my family, and my relationship with You. Amen

Acquire wisdom—how much better it is than gold! And acquire understanding—it is preferable to silver.

Proverbs 16:16 HCSB

ACQUIRING WISDOM

Proverbs 16:16 teaches us that wisdom is more valuable than gold. All of us would like to be wise, but not all of us are willing to do the work that is required to become wise. Wisdom is not like a mushroom; it does not spring up overnight. It is, instead, like an oak tree that starts as a tiny acorn, grows into a sapling, and eventually reaches up to the sky, tall and strong.

To become wise, we must seek God's wisdom and live according to His Word. To become wise, we must seek wisdom with consistency and purpose. To become wise, we must not only learn the lessons of the Christian life, we must also live by them.

Do you seek to live—and to lead—righteously and wisely? If so, you must study the ultimate source of wisdom: the Word of God. You must seek out worthy mentors and listen carefully to their advice. You must associate, day in and day out, with godly men and women. Then, as you accumulate wisdom, you must not keep it for yourself; you must, instead, share it with your friends, your family members, and your associates.

But be forewarned: if you sincerely seek to share your hard-earned wisdom with others, your actions must give credence to your words. The best way to share one's wisdom—perhaps the only way—is not by words, but by example.

— A LEADERSHIP TIP —

God makes His wisdom available to you. Your job is to acknowledge, to understand, and (above all) to use that wisdom.

Knowledge is horizontal. Wisdom is vertical; it comes down from above.

Billy Graham

God's plan for our guidance is for us to grow gradually in wisdom before we get to the cross roads.

Bill Hybels

— A LEADER'S PRAYER —

Dear Lord, when I trust in the wisdom of the world, I am often led astray, but when I trust in Your wisdom, I build my life upon a firm foundation. Today and every day I will trust Your Word and follow it, knowing that the ultimate wisdom is Your wisdom and the ultimate truth is Your truth. Amen

In fact, when we were with you, this is what we commanded you: "If anyone isn't willing to work, he should not eat."

2 Thessalonians 3:10 HCSB

WE'RE EXPECTED TO WORK

God's Word teaches us the value of hard work. In his second letter to the 2 Thessalonians, Paul warns, "If anyone isn't willing to work, he should not eat." And the Book of Proverbs proclaims, "One who is slack in his work is brother to one who destroys" (18:9 NIV). In short, God has created a world in which diligence is rewarded but sloth is not. So, whatever it is that you choose to do, do it with commitment, excitement, and vigor.

Hard work is not simply a proven way to get ahead; it's also part of God's plan for you. God did not create you for a life of mediocrity; He created you for far greater things. Reaching for greater things usually requires work and lots of it, which is perfectly fine with God. After all, He knows that you're up to the task, and He has big plans for you if you possess a loving heart and willing hands.

— A LEADERSHIP TIP —

When you find work that pleases God—and when you apply yourself conscientiously to the job at hand—you'll be rewarded.

We must trust as if it all depended on God and work as if it all depended on us.

C. H. Spurgeon

Thank God every morning when you get up that you have something which must be done, whether you like it or not. Work breeds a hundred virtues that idleness never knows.

Charles Kingsley

It may be that the day of judgment will dawn tomorrow; in that case, we shall gladly stop working for a better tomorrow. But not before.

Dietrich Bonhoeffer

The world does not consider labor a blessing, therefore it flees and hates it, but the pious who fear the Lord labor with a ready and cheerful heart, for they know God's command, and they acknowledge His calling.

Martin Luther

— A LEADER'S PRAYER —

Dear Lord, make my work pleasing to You. Help me to sow the seeds of Your abundance everywhere I go. Let me be diligent in all my undertakings and give me patience to wait for Your harvest. Amen

But seek first the kingdom of God and His righteousness, and all these things shall be added to you. Therefore do not worry about tomorrow, for tomorrow will worry about its own things. Sufficient for the day is its own trouble.

Matthew 6:33-34 NKJV

FAITHFUL LEADERS WORRY LESS

Because we are imperfect human beings struggling with imperfect circumstances, we worry. Even though we, as Christians, have the assurance of salvation—even though we, as Christians, have the promise of God's love and protection—we find ourselves fretting over the inevitable frustrations of everyday life. Jesus understood our concerns when He spoke the reassuring words found in the 6th chapter of Matthew.

Where is the best place to take your worries? Take them to God. Take your troubles to Him; take your fears to Him; take your doubts to Him; take your weaknesses to Him; take your sorrows to Him . . . and leave them all there. Seek protection from the One who offers you eternal salvation; build your spiritual house upon the Rock that cannot be moved.

Perhaps you are one of those leaders who worries about everything. If so, make Matthew 6 a regular part of your daily Bible reading. This beautiful passage will remind you that God still sits in His heaven and you are His beloved child. Then, perhaps, you will worry a little less and trust God a little more, and that's as it should be because God is trustworthy . . . and you are protected.

— A LEADERSHIP TIP —

Work hard, pray harder, and if you have any worries, take them to God—and leave them there.

The beginning of anxiety is the end of faith, and the beginning of true faith is the end of anxiety.

George Mueller

Worry is the senseless process of cluttering up tomorrow's opportunities with leftover problems from today.

Barbara Johnson

— A LEADER'S PRAYER —

Dear Lord, wherever I find myself, let me celebrate more and worry less. When my faith begins to waver, help me to trust You more. Then, with praise on my lips and the love of Your Son in my heart, let me live courageously, faithfully, prayerfully, and thankfully this day and every day. Amen

I was glad when they said unto me, let us go into the house of the LORD.

Psalm 122:1 KJV

OUR NEED TO WORSHIP GOD

All of humanity is engaged in worship. The question is not whether we worship, but what we worship. Wise men and women choose to worship God. When they do, they are blessed with a plentiful harvest of joy, peace, and abundance. Other people choose to distance themselves from God by foolishly worshiping things that are intended to bring personal gratification but not spiritual gratification. Such choices often have tragic consequences.

If we place our love for material possessions above our love for God—or if we yield to the countless temptations of this world—we find ourselves engaged in a struggle between good and evil, a clash between God and Satan. Our responses to these struggles have implications that echo throughout our families and throughout our communities.

How can we ensure that we cast our lot with God? We do so, in part, by the practice of regular, purposeful worship in the company of fellow believers. When we worship God faithfully and fervently, we are blessed. When we fail to worship God, for whatever reason, we forfeit the spiritual gifts that He intends for us.

We must worship our Heavenly Father, not just with our words, but also with deeds. We must honor Him, praise Him, and obey Him. As we seek to find purpose and meaning for our lives, we must first seek His purpose and His will. For believers, God comes first. Always first.

— A LEADERSHIP TIP —

When you worship God with a sincere heart, He will guide your steps and bless your life.

I am of the opinion that we should not be concerned about working for God until we have learned the meaning and delight of worshipping Him.

A. W. Tozer

When God is at the center of your life, you worship. When he's not, you worry.

Rick Warren

— A LEADER'S PRAYER —

Dear Lord, this world is a place of distractions and temptations. But when I worship You, Father, You set my path—and my heart—straight. Let this day and every day be a time of worship. Help me find quiet moments to praise You for Your blessings, for Your love, and for Your Son. Amen

TRUST THE LORD
WITH ALL YOUR HEART,
AND DON'T DEPEND ON
YOUR OWN UNDERSTANDING.
REMEMBER THE LORD
IN ALL YOU DO,
AND HE WILL GIVE YOU SUCCESS.

—

PROVERBS 3:5-6 NCV